These fragments I have shored against my ruins
T. S. Eliot, *The Watershed*

Remembering
Tommy Waldron, Joe Dunn,
Ciaran Fahey and Padraig (P. V.) O'Brien.
Formative friends for fragmentary times.

Maynooth College is two hundred years old. Age is honourable and achievement is to be honoured, and both age and achievement will be widely celebrated on the bicentenary. The occasion will see the celebration of Maynooth's original purpose, still continued, the training of priests for Ireland. It will also mark the development of that purpose over two centuries, eventually to include third-level education of men and women in philosophy and theology, in the sciences, and in the arts.

To honour in an appropriate way these two hundred years of teaching, members of the college staff are publishing a series of books in a number of academic disciplines. Edited by members of the College Faculty, these books will range from texts based on standard theology courses to interdisciplinary studies with a theological or religious involvement.

The venture is undertaken with pride in the long Maynooth academic tradition and in modest continuance of it.

Editorial Board:

Patrick Hannon
Ronan Drury
Gerard Watson

Contents

CHAPTER ONE

In a dark and fragmentary time

Millennial fears mislead. They focus foolishly on texts and figures that are opaque in themselves and in their relationships. Jubilee celebrations may be no more justified if they reflect a Christian or Western triumphalism too often experienced as conquering power. Repentance (*metanoia*) may be a more apt attitude for Christians than celebration. Repentance may be the celebration.

This is not a book about millennium or jubilee, although it is about church and society in the last decade of this century, which has proved a dark and fragmentary time for both. Church and society globally and locally, in the world at large and in Ireland, are beset by new and improved violence, division and despair. Ireland and the Catholic Church in Ireland might well be paradigm cases of how the darkness and fragmentation prevail and are yet qualified by fresh or persisting elements of light and connectedness. At least theological reflection of the Irish case-history may help confirm or correct reflections and conclusions derived from a broader base. The future of world society and of the world church is always dependent on the present of local societies and local churches. Sarajevo and Clonmacnoise in their times deeply affect the future of Europe, socially and ecclesially.

The primary concerns here are the Irish church and Christian faith in Part I, and the interaction of faith and society in Part II. The theological reflections and responses in Part I were prompted by occasions and invitations over years in which a church crisis in Ireland was manifest. In Part II the Irish crisis is presumed in the background but the concerns are more clearly global and the approach more explicitly hopeful, almost as if the journey beyond darkness and fragmentation needed to transcend this tiny island and encircle the created and redeemed world.

A Church Fragmenting in a Fragmenting Society

Contemporary Ireland is to many observers the first successful

Ireland. It is Modern Ireland. Modernisation in technology, economics, law and politics, in social mores and cultural tastes, has followed a little belatedly and a little differently the example of its
European partners and North American leaders. But not without
the shadow side of all such changes. Because of the rapidity of the
changes in Ireland, a century and more crammed into thirty years,
and because of the quite different points of departure, the shadows
can seem deeper and longer.

The much-needed and much-vaunted economic progress, head-
ing the European league for a number of years, has made little
impact on overall unemployment and none at all on the long-term
unemployed. Thirty percent of the population is still stuck at or
below the poverty-line with all the attendant disadvantages in
healthcare, education and real participation in the society.
Meantime the gap between the seriously rich and the rest of the
population continues to widen.

For all the admirable peace-processing, the Northern 'troubles'
continue to disturb minds, destroy lives and consume badly needed
energy and resources. In parallel there has emerged Ireland's first
organised crime system, involving drug-barons, gang feuds, hit-
men and assassinations, culminating in June 1996 in the assassin-
ation of journalist Veronica Guerin on the open road. Other crimes
of violence against the elderly, the isolated, teenagers and a range
of women victims, with increasing numbers of physical and sexual
attacks on children, make the daily newspaper read like an anthology
of crime.

These problems are not the effects of the modernisation process
which has protected human rights, promoted tolerance and, certainly in its earlier stages, increased or even established participation in governing society. There is so much, old and new, that is
valuable in Irish society in terms of personal and community relations, in caring for the elderly, the sick and the poor, in developing
attractive towns and countryside, in the spread of education, in
commitment by so many to the peoples of the developing world, in
the creative resurgence in music, literature and all the arts, that it
must seem churlish to go on about the problems. The problems do
happen to be the 'bad companions' of modern Ireland with parallels elsewhere and may owe something to the individualism and
pressure for economic success (by any means?) which modernisation can occasion. They have also their roots in the weaknesses of
premodern Irish society, from intolerant nationalism or unionism,

to land-hunger, to family-violence and discrimination against women. Without, however, attempting any more detailed and finely balanced sketch of Irish society, or allocating blame, it can be safely maintained that Ireland is a seriously disturbed society in transition. It is in that context the Catholic Church must be discussed now and will be examined more closely later in this book.

Official and unofficial Catholic spokespeople have proved over the years the most vocal critics of the modernisation of Ireland. The bitter referenda debates on divorce and abortion of the 1980s and 1990s made that clear. Of course certain aspects of the modernisation project were supported at official church level where greater justice for the poor or opposition to violence were concerned. Many Catholic clergy, and in the end a majority of Catholic lay-people, supported the developments in general and in the specific details from women's rights to the legalisation of homosexuality. Yet the Catholic Church was presented and often presented itself as the main opposition to the emergence of a modern Ireland. In doing so it sometimes offered some acute and much needed analysis and critique of policies which ignored already neglected peoples and religions. Even that valuable critique was increasingly undermined by its own divisions on many of the issues, its treatment of its vulnerable and different and, above all, in recent years by the series of sexual and other abuse scandals which have been exposed among the clergy and religious. The marked decline in vocations to the priesthood and religious life, and the slower decline in church attendance, had anticipated the emergence of these scandals. The scandals did accelerate the processes of decline. More serious still have been the often fumbling and ineffectual attempts by church leadership to deal with these difficulties. A church fragmenting does not seem too harsh a description of the present state of the Irish Catholic Church given the various declines and divisions. It has its parallels, more or less close, among other churches and in Catholic churches across the world.

Disintegration or Restoration?

Earlier fears and warnings of church leaders and other church members about the decline in Irish society have to focus more directly now on the decline or even disintegration of the church. The continuing scandals, the divisions on internal church matters like a married priesthood or the ordination of women, the divisions on external affairs in relation to other churches and to society, the

dissatisfaction with the leadership of the church and increasing sec-
ularisation of society, suggest a system spinning out of control.
While there are many low-level initiatives which reflect the church
at its best and in serious pursuit of renewal, there is little evidence
of a vision at the top that would awaken and harness the undoubtedly enormous but dormant resources which the believing people
of Ireland still possess. Recourse to old and tired language and
ideas predominates. Evangelisation may be intended to bring the
good and the new but the mindset evident in some recent church
proposals in Ireland and elsewhere suggests a recycling of the old
and the failed. Re-storation rather than re-newal seems the final
remedy. Re-pentance, the biblical transformation of hearts and
minds, of attitudes, activities and structures, has not yet captured
the imagination of the Irish church. Until it does the decline will
continue into disintegration, the winter darkness which the church
has experienced for some years will prevail, despite some occasional
flashes of artificial or even real light.

Taking the Darkness Seriously

Lumen Gentium, light to the peoples of the world, opened a key text
and formed a key slogan of Vatican II. *Tenebrae Gentium* would not
have matched just then the mood or the reality. For the prophets of
doom, the modern world was all *tenebrae*, all darkness. For the
Johannine visionaries, renewal of the church involved appreciating
and learning from the same world. Yet for them also the church
should and would be the light of the world. Light and darkness
have come and gone for church and world in the intervening
decades. For now, Irish Catholics and Christians are called to take
their own darkness seriously.

In revealing the darker side of clerical and church life, recent sex
and other abuse cases were important reminders of that darkness. It
is obviously a darkness of human weakness and sin which ultimately affects all church members.

Yielding to the temptation to scapegoat particular priests or sisters or brothers who are known to have failed, would obscure the
solidarity of all in darkness and in sin. The publicly known are all
Christian brothers and sisters, fellow members of the Body of Christ
and colleagues in the 'clerical' church. As the grace and light are
shared, so are the sin and the darkness. Recognising and accepting
the darkness which embraces the whole church is a current call. It is
not a darkness produced by simply sexual failure, another tempt-

ingly evasive route. The darkness and sin of the church pervades all
its human dimensions and is manifest in all manner of human sin-
ning. Pride and power may be much more insidious sources of
church sin than sexual weakness. Of course the three may be closely
intertwined in the personal and institutional failures just experienced. Pride and power often prevented acknowledgement of what
was truly happening in the actual abuse cases. They delayed effective response and now seem likely to inhibit, if not finally prevent,
the radical revision of the clerical structures of the church which is
so long overdue.

The darkness reaches further and deeper than the obvious failures of church leaders and members. It is a feature of humanity
itself from which Christians can deceive themselves that they are
escaping. In origin and destiny, in self-awareness and self-develop-
ment, in person and in community, human beings constantly
encounter their darkness. For all the discoveries of the physical and
human sciences, for all the insights of artists, philosophers and
theologians, the wall of darkness encompassing humanity and
nature looms suddenly and fearfully. Distractions and deceptions
abound together with the real discoveries. The darkness persists to
its final certainty in death of self or friend, of civilisation or even
planet.

Faith, trust in the God of light, appears to offer the ultimate triumph over the darkness of creatures and creation. For many it is an
empty offer, a childish evasion. For Christians also and their religious ancestors, the Jews, God is not readily a God of light, at least
not a God of accessible light. Master of faith Moses had to enter the
darkness to meet his God on Mount Sinai. Job's experience of the
darkness of God is a type of how many humans struggle. The darkness of the 'abandoned' Jesus of Calvary spread over the face of the
earth. And central to the great mystical tradition of Christianity is
the dark night of the soul. God's darkness is part of the experience
of his most graced and committed devotees. Taking the darkness
seriously means taking the darkness of God seriously beyond shallow, superstitious manifestations and even beyond established formulae and canonised practices. The Christian community, with its
traditions of belief and practice, provides a context for encounter
with God, but always in the consciousness of human and divine
darkness.

A Generative Darkness

Creation and new life are closely associated with darkness and dying in human and religious traditions. In its original created state 'the earth was without form, and void, and darkness was upon the face of the deep', according to Genesis 1. As the Spirit moved upon the face of the waters, creation took form and shape, finally living form and human shape. In the forming of Israel the rhythm of darkness and light, of life and death and life continued. When 'Christ Jesus, being in the form of God ... took upon himself the form of a servant, and was made in the likeness of men ... he humbled himself and became obedient unto death, even the death of the cross' (Phil 2:6-8), and so passed over to new life in resurrection. All this is anticipated in the gospel accounts of his life and his teaching. 'Unless the seed falling into the ground die ...'. 'Only he who loses his life shall save it'. 'Greater love than this no one has than that he lay down his life for his friends.' Out of the darkness of dying and death comes new life but it has to be taken on willingly in human terms and accepted fully and disintegratingly by seed and human.

The present darkness of the church, or more particularly of the Irish church, is not the first in history. Indeed the darkness has never been far away. What is significant and perhaps providential at present is the accumulation of obstacles to the light, obstacles originating in the church, such as clerical sexual abuse and abuse of power, and obstacles originating without, but operative within, like the disappearance of value and meaning and the frenzied search for alternatives in pleasure or possessions. Accepting the present darkness as no mere transient phenomenon, but as the result of long development, and entering through it into the more critical darknesses of humanity, creation and God, the church begins to germinate seeds anew. The darkness of death will yield to the light and life of resurrection.

Strangers in the Dark

Emphasis on the dark may not only be depressing for many people, it may also seem self-indulgent and deliberately mystifying. Taking the darkness so seriously may be another strategy of evasion of the real problem and real resources of the church. It would help to move from the abstractions of darkness to some of the more concrete expressions of it. Things are different in the dark. People are different. Familiars become strangers. 'Who goes there?' From gospel to Shakespeare, to children's story, strangers and the dark belong together, the dark of soul as well as of body. On the road to Emmaus the eyes of two disciples were held so that they did not recognise the stranger who joined them. In every human life every-body is stranger to begin with, including mother and child. Estrangement between husband and wife, between parents and children, is part of the process of development. Defamiliarisation and the darkness that precedes or accompanies it, is a common per-sonal and social process. The process reflects a deeper darkness and strangeness. To speak of 'strangers' may be at once more precise and more threatening than to speak of 'others'. The other has played a very valuable role in recent philosophical and theological discussion. The work of Otto and Levinas, of Ricoeur and Tracy, has been especially helpful in exploring faith and ethics, in develop-ing a language of the transcendent in a secular age. The other, human and divine, created and uncreated, and the stranger are closely related in contemporary theological usage and in biblical background. The stranger is the preferred term here and elsewhere in this book as more illuminating of the particular human and eccles-ial predicaments addressed. The sinister note which strangers can convey reflects better the darker time. The strange and the stranger may be experienced first as threat, and that threatening shadow side never quite disappears for husbands and wives, parents and children, friends and neighbours, colleagues and competitors. At intertribal, international and inter-church levels, the threatening and shadow side can be powerfully persistent.

The strangers encountered are first of all other human beings with their unknown qualities and unpredictable behaviour. Their opacity or darkness in this way is never finally removed even in the closest and most enduring relationship. No relationship is ever completely safe in the sense that it is never complete. On both sides there are unknown and unrealised potentials and threats. As there are many relationships in anybody's life the incompleteness is spread and the insecurity deepened. Each person is an uneasy coali-tion of relationships and causes, developments and potentials, which are not fully transparent to the self. The stranger within each human self is as important as the stranger without. As already hinted, the strangeness of the other and of the self is a source, a necessary source, of growth and understanding as well as darkness and threat. It is gift as well as threat, but unless the strangeness and the accompanying darkness are attended to, the gift will be ignored or frustrated. The darkness and strangeness which recent events in the church have manifested may, if taken seriously, be the way to exposing fresh aspects of the gift of the church, may be the way to renewal.

Human Strangers and the Strangeness of God

For many, the church crisis in Ireland and elsewhere is but a symptom of a faith crisis, of a God crisis. The philosophical and theological attention to the other is an attempt to deal with this crisis. Human and created otherness, in relationship and in response, may through reflection and analysis reveal or at least point towards unconditional, ultimate and uncreated otherness. It may help with the recovery of the transcendent within creation. The strangeness of humans and of all creatures could play a similar role. The stranger approach would have its own advantages and disadvantages, its own ambiguities in understanding and response, the weaknesses of its strengths. The persisting strangeness of human beings and of creation, with its overhang of threat, induces an awe combining wonder and fear. The gift and threat of the strange and the stranger belong together. The human need and call is to enable the gift to triumph over the threat. It is a life-long, never to be completed task. Yet the gratuitous presence and unconditional call of the human stranger to recognition and response, opens up to the ultimate strangeness in reality, a presence that is awesome, wonderful and fearful, the gift and threat of the stranger God.

Estrangement, Exclusion and 'Scapegoating'

The triumph of threat over gift between human strangers issues in estrangement between persons and communities. Child abuse, recently and savagely exposed in the Irish church and in Irish society, is a particularly disturbing expression of the triumph of threat. The innocence, the trust and the power, so destructively exploited in these events, estrange not only abusers and abused in very profound ways; they affect whole societies. The regular and reasonable reaction of the abused and her society is angry exclusion of the abuser. As the legal forms are followed, the abuser if convicted enters society's symbolic exclusion zone of the convicted criminal and its physical exclusion zone of prison.

Human estrangement and its exclusion zones can have deeper implications for excluding and excluded. The excluded may have to carry the further burden of the unrecognised or denied destructiveness of the excluding. The demonising of the excluded sex-offenders or political terrorists or other criminals as utterly evil, sometimes covers fear of the evil in oneself. Their banishment by excommunication or exile, by imprisonment or death, may be due to the threat of the criminals to the self. The widespread human practice of scapegoating is alive and well in church and society. Just now clergy guilty of sex-abuse may be conveniently scapegoated in church. In Irish society the clerical church, male and female, provides a plausible excuse for a range of ills in the aftermath of its decades of hegemony. The church as scapegoat has replaced the British or the politicians or the government or other readily demonised figures and institutions.

In the Book of Leviticus (Ch 16), the sins of the people were laid upon a goat who was then expelled into the desert. The Christ who became 'sin for us' could be interpreted on one level in this way. However, as Rene Girard has insisted, the thrust of the Judeo-Christian tradition is to expose the fallacy of more ancient pagan traditions whereby people avoided responsibility for their own sins by 'scapegoating'. The totally innocent victim Jesus Christ summons and enables humanity to confront and confess its own internal sinfulness, personal and social. Only thereby is it cleansed. Accepting the sinful strangeness of the self is integral to reconciling rather than demonising the sinful strangers about us.

Faith in Fragments

The estrangements, with their mutual exclusions and excommunications in person, church and society, lead to very fragmented lives for all. 'Fragmented' is a key term and not just a modish one. The breaches and brokenness it describes are sharp, mulitple and untidy at the edges. No amount of PR or political or theological rhetoric can conceal this fragmentation. No simply human efforts can overcome it. Personal dying, the most obvious and the definitive case of personal and relational fragmentation, has its analogues in political, social and cultural disintegration. In human terms, the church is a history of periodic estrangements and fragmentations. Its presence to the world just as now as Roman Catholic, or more broadly Christian, is marked by division and disagreement.

Fragmented Christian communities involve fragmented believers. In relationship to God and to Jesus Christ, they share the brokenness of the rest of their relationships. They enjoy at best a partially broken faith in its relational dynamic and its credal content. Even as they say the creed together so many do not understand what they may be assenting to and do not assent to what they may be understanding. Theirs is indeed a faith in fragments.

For many Christians today, accepting personally the full range of Christian beliefs, as they are in so many ways so well represented in the new Catholic Catechism, is beyond their capacity. To suggest that they simply accept all such formulations in obedience to the church is to ignore the difficulties and difference in church formulations and their own role in working through these difficulties. More seriously, it would undermine the authenticity of their personal commitment to the God who trancends all formulae.

Fragments in Communion

How is faith possible at all then? It was, of course, never easy, as Jesus' warnings in the gospels confirm. Today and perhaps always it is faith in fragments and in community. This may seem self-contradictory. Unity and community are imcompatible with fragmentation. Not quite and not in history. In history, indeed, communities from family to nation to church are formed from uneasy and unstable combinations of fragments. So are individual persons in their physical make-up and their psychic and social lives.

The witness and life of the community-church, for all its divisions and failure, can still provide a context for relating to the ultimate mystery of life as manifest and lived out in Jesus Christ. In that context, all kinds of fragments of truths and justice and freedom, of gift and threat, of failure, forgiveness and reconciliation, may confirm or provoke a fresh sense of that mystery in Jesus Christ, a fresh impetus to hope and love for human beings and so to fresh faith in God. The fragments can and should provide the way into fuller faith and not the way out.

Of course the historical community of the church is unstable; the fragment frequently opaque or contradictory; faith a hazardous journey. But then it is not primarily a human achievement. The ultimately believing self, the faith provoking fragments encountered in the others, the continuing if fragile community of belief, are primarily gift. The search for and the recognition of the mysterious giver are called faith.

History is fragmentation. Completion is called eschatology, the final gift of the mystery. Personal dying is, in Christian terms, a bringing together of the fragments of a life often scattered over many years, relationships and communities, achievements and failures. The loving and beloved child or the dying friendless tycoon may be rescued and integrated into a fullness of potential by the receiving God of resurrection. Resurrection, personal, relational and communal, is God's way of overcoming fragmentation through fulfilment in communion. That that way of God's involves fatal fragmentation is the key fragment of Christian belief, the death and resurrection of Jesus Christ.

The recent exposures of clerical sexual scandals and of other weaknesses in the church was genuinely surprising and shocking to many Irish people. God was not surprised or shocked. This church, suddenly revealed in all its shamefulness, was the church as God knew it. It was the church as God loved it. The vision of God penetrated the veils of respectability and secrecy drawn over the human failures of the church. This is the healing vision of God. Divine judgement, which exposure also involves, is only a way to divine forgiveness. Justice, not to be denied, is subsumed in mercy and love. Fragments of human faith and goodness are finally taken up into the transforming communion of the trinitarian God 'saved in hope'.

It is in the spirit of some such hope that these fragments of five painful years are brought together in this book.

PART I

A Fragmentary Church

CHAPTER TWO

Ten questions for the Irish Catholic Church

June 1992

Events in Irish life over the last year suggest, even at the distance of New York, some upheaval in Ireland and in its civil and religious self-understanding which may take years to appreciate. To many observers and analysts, both of Ireland and of its wider context, these events were more dramatic instances of (partly hidden) movements in Irish society which broke surface in that extraordinary period of September 1991 to May 1992. What may yet follow is impossible to predict.

Given the history of their development and the tangled nature of these issues, instant diagnosis and prescription are simply not possible. For the Irish Catholic Church, a period of prayer and reflection, involving all of us in repentance and conversion, is clearly required. Yet such exercises have their own ambiguity unless they are conducted in an open and communal way, with expressions of prayer and repentance reinforced by honest intellectual struggle with the real sources of our malaise. The evasion of serious intellectual debate, a perennial temptation in Ireland, can only compound our problems.

To assist this reflection and debate, some outline headings in the form of questions are offered here. They are not the only possible questions. Neither are they necessarily the best ones. And they leave many significant areas of Catholic and Christian concern untouched.

To clarify the discussion, it is important that we restrict the use of the word 'church' to denote the whole church, and avoid using it to denote particular groups within the church, such as the bishops or the clergy or the religious or the laity.

1. Could the whole Irish Catholic Church recognise clearly and persistently its responsibility to the financial, political and broader social moral standards of its members as well as to their sexual moral standards? It may be true that priests seldom preach on sex these days, or that Catholic teachers and parents in the main ignore it, but the overall moral ethos of the country, as well as recent events, suggests a much greater preoccupation with sexual morality than with truth or justice or reconciliation.

2. How should the Irish Catholic bishops acknowledge their shared responsibility with priests, religious and laity in analysing and responding to the present crisis? Can they do that effectively without serious and open pastoral consultation in their dioceses and parishes?

3. Can the regular meetings of Irish Catholic bishops ever hope to understand properly, and respond effectively to, the challenges of the Irish Catholic Church without real participation by a range of consultors, lay, religious and clerical; theological, professional and pastoral?

4. Can issues of financial morality be addressed by the whole Irish Catholic Church without complete openness about church finances? Where they come from? How they are protected and invested? How they are spent?

5. Can the issues of political morality be addressed without openness about the politics within the church structures in regard to the appointment of bishops and to the making of episcopal decisions which directly affect the people?

6. How can issues of sexual morality be addressed without the participation of laity (married and single), priests, sisters and brothers, theologians, psychologists, therapists and other experts? How is the present gap between teaching and practice in regard, for example, to contraception, to be honestly handled?

7. How far is obligatory rather than optional celibacy necessary or helpful for the diocesan clergy in the fulfilment of its mission today? How far is it possible for many? Meantime, what of friendships between priests and women?

8. How are women to be integrated fully into the membership and the mission of the Irish Catholic Church? How are present injustices to be overcome? How far are they related to the question of ordination? How is this question to be properly debated in the whole church?

9. More profoundly and centrally, how is the gospel of Jesus Christ to be preached and lived in Irish society today in face of the diminishing credibility of message and messenger?

10. Can the Irish Catholic Church take up this challenge effectively without humbly seeking the help of its Christian sisters and brothers in other churches?

Some of these questions need immediate response. Others of them will require further analysis and discussion by the whole Irish Catholic Church over the next years. The present anxious period may be the *kairos*, the God-given time and challenge we have needed to move towards a transformed Irish Church in what is becoming a rapidly and radically transformed Irish society.

CHAPTER THREE

The winter name of church

January 1995

The pain-lines of the Brendan Smyth affair run their savage way throughout the island of Ireland. Most deeply and painfully damaged are the child-abuse victims themselves and their families. Their healing will be slow and difficult. They have so many companions in suffering whose plight is only emerging, and many more whose plight may never emerge. In the coming months and years, Ireland, like many countries, will have to confront the secret suffering of its abused children and the secret shame of its child-abusers. To do this in an honest, healing or redemptive way will test its personal and social resources to the limit.

Beyond the victims and their families, the damage to a range of people and institutions, while less immediately painful, is still enormous. Government, the judiciary, politics and the legal system have been diminished in credibility and authority. The healing and restoration will be slow and painful for these persons and institutions also. However, the parliamentary and judicial systems have some self-reforming mechanisms which will help, although only an informed and committed citizenry can ensure these mechanisms work. Such reform is a small but essential part of what society owes to its sex-abuse victims and others who have suffered from the recent negligence, incompetence and corruption in state institutions.

The Brendan Smyth affair, with its dramatic exposure of child-abuse, casts longer shadows still. The darkness reaches into the most intimate and trusting of Irish community relationships in family, school and church. This has not been a recent or sudden descent into darkness. The current public list of cases goes back over a generation. Experienced counsellors and confessors could attest to a much longer history. That history had tangled roots in moral, psychological, social and material privation. These have been compounded by sexual miseducation, general human weakness, as well as deliberate self-indulgence at the expense of the dependent and manipulable. The social and educational reforms, for which the present revelations and their antecedents call, far exceed those required in politics and law. And many of them are required for reasons other than that of child sexual abuse, harrowing and urgent as that cause is.

Abuse of trust

For very many people, the greatest shock of recent sad events was that Brendan Smyth, the convicted child abuser, was a priest. The shock was mixed with anger at the handling of the case by authorities in both church and state. Church authorities seemed to some to be grossly negligent in not following through on early complaints. Invoking the niceties of ecclesiastical jurisdiction, however valuable in other contexts, was considered inadequate to the moral demands of repeated complaints. Excuses based on ignorance of the serious consequences for the victims appeared too self-serving. The admission of mistakes and the promise of safeguards for the future sounded weak to genuinely dismayed Catholics and sympathetic others, as well as to those who might be secretly or openly delighted at the embarrassment to the church.

The further complications of the unexplained delay in dealing with the extradition, and the continuing suspicion that this was due to the fact that Brendan Smyth was a priest, and to the possibility that some church influence was at work, has damaged church authority and credibility still further. Stories that somebody in the Attorney General's office, or the AG himself, were members of Opus Dei or of the Knights of Columbanus, and that this influenced their judgment, may be only malicious rumours. They persist and continue to damage the church's reputation. The Dáil investigation, about to get under way, may prove them to be false. It will not relieve the church's long-term difficulty with 'clandestine' organisations operating in its supposed interest.

The dismay at the involvement of a priest in child-abuse derived properly from the special degree of trust which characterised relationships between priests, families and children in Ireland for so long. However small the percentage of child-abusers who turn out to be priests or religious, the damage to that traditional trust is serious and long-lasting. Other professional/pastoral relationships may be damaged as fresh stories emerge, but few if any enjoyed the same taken-for-granted freedom from suspicion as the relationship of priest and child.

The priest's freedom from suspicion of sexual involvement has been dented over the years as far as adults were concerned. Indeed there was a lot of sympathy among Catholics for priests who feel in love or got sexually involved with a parishioner or friend. Some reactions at the time to the resignation of Bishop Eamonn Casey reflected this sympathy. The sympathy is inevitably less where the break-up of a marriage follows. It is also more ambiguous where the relationship is homosexual. The death of a priest in a gay club in the midst of the Brendan Smyth affair reinforced the scandal at one level, while permitting parish grief and clerical, even episcopal, participation in the mourning. To the actions of the 'paedophile priest' the response was unambiguous. Exploitation of children by any adult, and above all by one in such a privileged position of trust, should not be tolerated or excused. The excusing cause of consenting adults did not arise.

Trust, celibacy and holiness

The pastoral privileges of the priest have, in the Roman Catholic tradition, certainly in Ireland, been closely associated with celibacy. Unmarried for the sake of the Kingdom of God seemed to offer not only a release from the usual cares of family life, but also from the usual sexual drives. Perfect chastity, as it used to be called, was presumed, temptation barely discussed, and 'deviance' unthinkable. Of course it was never quite like that inside or outside the clerical world. Even in the 1950s seminarians were duly warned and priests were subject to gossip about the houses and people they frequented. While much of the warning and gossip was lacking in substance, and Irish people were willing to believe the best of their priests, they did not all need Graham Greene or even John Broderick to remind them of a priest's sexual vulnerability. Some were insightful enough to recosnise a priest's own scrupulosity as inability to come to terms with his sexuality or to see in his usually covert resort to alcohol a symtom of the same difficulty.

Despite these proper cautions, Irish people did respect the celibacy of their priests and believed that priests respected it themselves. And for the most part they did, even if it caused much personal pain. Some of the pain came from a lack of self-understanding. Sexual self-understanding does not come easily even to happily married people. It is undoubtedly more difficult for the single and the celibate. If one were to judge by the sexual attitudes and practices of either the 'repressed' or the 'liberated', sexual maturity and

the implied self-understanding may be only slowly and with difficulty achieved at all. Such judgment would, however, pre-empt the
kind of debate and education which this crisis requires. And it dis-
tracts from the immediate point at issue – the trust which a celibate
clergy enjoyed and which now seems betrayed.

Trust enjoyed and trust betrayed are not quickly restored, as
many priests can already report. So it should be. The valuable and
trustworthy role which so many priests still play in Irish life does
not mean that that trust can be maintained without fresh effort. In a
situation of betrayal, even by the few, trust must be earned anew.
That is simply part of the Christian call. Yet further differentiation
is needed in discussing the connection between pastoral trust and a
celibate clergy.

Celibacy was often too readily associated with holiness. There
was an anti-body, anti-sex and, for many commentators, anti-
woman element at work here, an element much older and wider
than clerical celibacy or indeed Christianity itself. The holy was the
spiritual as opposed to the bodily and especially the sexual. Women
were, in men's eyes and desires, the bodily and the sexual. This
vision of holiness was puritan. Distance from the bodily ensured
closeness to the divine, a very unstable position for a religion that
had at its centre God made flesh. It would seem to be particularly at
odds with a religious belief and community that was strongly
sacramental, that even regarded the sexual commitment and communion of man and woman as a sacrament, unlike the commitment
of celibacy. This spiritual and intellectual ambiguity persists for
many Christians and Catholics. On its shadow side, it can pose
unreal expectations in sexual morality and exaggerate sexual failure over other moral failures. It does not, however, diminish the
responsibility of those who undertake celibacy to make a serious
effort to live it or leave it. But celibacy in itself does not betoken
holiness, and the vast majority of people called to holiness are not
called to celibacy.

The holiness, the sense of the Holy, of God, which Christians
and others expect from their leaders and ministers is related to their
lifestyle, or rather their love-style. Celibacy may reinforce this for
some ministers and for some of the ministered to. That it is not a
divine but a human requirement of priestly ministry is self-evident.
That the present scandals, even of the few, raise questions about the
value and possibility of an exclusively celibate priesthood in the
Roman Catholic Church is equally evident. Yet it is not the scandals

which are of first importance in this debate. They have a longer history than 1990s Ireland and its antecedents. What needs to be discussed is how far even the best male celibate priesthood can produce a balanced leadership in the church. Can it adequately reflect the human and cosmic universality of the incarnation and redemption accomplished in the Word made flesh, in the divine become human and so sexual and cosmic? If the present debate is to get beyond the necessary exchanges in the popular media, a good deal of hard thinking on such issues will be called for from Irish Catholics and Christians. The reluctance to think, to grapple honestly and freely with these deeper issues, may be a much more serious cause of present church confusion and future decline than clerical scandals.

A couple of deeper but related issues deserve brief consideration here, at least to alert church-members to the need for further hard thinking. The celibate-as-holier tendency has fed into false distinctions between this-worldly and other-worldly and between the profane or secular and the sacred. The conflict between the 'religious right' and the 'secular left' in Ireland and elsewhere is to some extent a war of phoney ideas, although the power struggle may be very real. For its own sake and that of society, the church needs to help sort out these phoney ideas before the country is plunged into further crises about abortion, schooling, and so on. The crisis of the church in Ireland, and the wider crisis, is certainly an intellectual one and demands all the intellectual resources, values and virtues available.

The complex relations of the puritan, the celibate and the holy shift once more, in the context of sin and grace, of fall and repentance, to conversion. Jesus spent time with sinners. They would go first into the Kingdom. They were open to his call and his saving grace. The self-righteous, the self-sufficient and the self-enclosing religious leaders cut themselves off from the presence and the power of the God who was healing and transforming love. They were not the only religious people to do so in human history. Successors abound. The assumption of the high moral ground is a widespread temptation, and outside religious institutions also. It can easily leave the assumers stranded with their own attempts at self-justification. This can only end in self-destruction or humiliation or both. The community of Jesus' disciples must recognise their own continuing sinfulness and so must their priestly leaders if Jesus' saving grace is to get through. The pedestal role of priests was always unreal and dangerous. The old seminary slogan that

only a holy priest makes a holy people was always in need of the
balance that only a holy people makes a holy priest. It may be easier
to accept now that sin and holiness overlap in everybody and that it
is only priests and people, humbly recognising their sinfulness
together, who can be made holy by Jesus Christ and by each other.

Suffering and Darkness

At the heart of holy-making lies suffering, one's own, other people's, the suffering of Jesus Christ. This is part of the scandal of
Christian faith, as Paul knew so well. It is part of all faith in a loving
God, as Job identified so clearly. That the painful suffering of sexual
abuse should be inflicted on the powerless by people they would
regard as representatives of the loving God moves well beyond
stumbling block (*skandalon*). *Skotos* (darkness) rather than *skandalon*
might be the more appropriate biblical term. A sense of darkness, of
winter darkness, of the darkness of death, has surrounded recent
revelations. In Ireland it is said that the old church is dying. (The
old politics may be dying also.) And more to come: scandals, darkness, death. Above all, more suffering to be inflicted and to be
endured.

There are frightening precedents of Christian infliction of suffering, even in the name of God, from Charlemagne's conversion programme, to the Inquisition, to the mutual martyrdoms of the
Reformation period. The complicity of so many Christians in the
Jewish Holocaust in this century reveals how deeply the urge to
destroy the neighbour is rooted in the history and psyche of those
who see themselves as called to love him. The darkness of such suffering is not recent and not especially Irish or Catholic. But it is that
now, and Irish Catholics have to recognise it as theirs. In this they
need leadership. It must be leadership from within the community
of the suffering. The failure to follow through on complaints was
finally the Christian failure to share that suffering while initiating
moves to help prevent and to heal.

As the darkness deepens, and it will, with a backlog of real (and
imagined) cases of sexual abuse, false dawns and easy solutions
may prove irresistable. Simple analysis concentrating on the sexual
difficulties of the few may prove readily acceptable. Better screen-
ing, better formation, better support and management of the clergy,
will remove the few 'bad apples' in time. The real crisis may thus be
evaded, the true darkness unrecognised. Clerical paedophilia and
other sexual failures signal deeper darkness and more widespread

suffering in the larger body of the church. The darkness of mind and spirit in the community-church frequently remains unrecognised at the level of bishops and priests because they have not absorbed the suffering that causes and is caused by the darkness. The fine pastoral words that speak of poverty and justice, of respect for life and marital love, do not reach the poor and oppressed, the unhappily married and the desperately pregnant. They do not change the oppressors and tormentors. The refiners of these words are too protected from the darkness and suffering. They will need to enter more deeply into the darkness of their people and let themselves be inhabited by their suffering.

Entering the Darkness

There are bishops, priests and religious, especially women religious, who have sought to share this darkness and suffering. More radical and more widespread sharing is called for. It will not be easy to achieve. Apart from their personal reluctance to leave their accustomed and comfortable material, mental and spiritual lives, they may not be at all welcome. Admission to these circles of darkness and suffering has to be earned. Recognising the true darkness and the church's contribution to it, by its fine words and unbreachable power-structures, may demand more than many of us are able for. Important gestures of goodwill, involving symbolic and real acts of renunciation, can prepare the way. The fripperies of office, from mitres to first place at the table, could be easily and rapidly left aside. More difficult will be the style of power, particularly the style of teaching power, which at present owes so little to learning from the Spirit among the people. The long-term listening demanded, after so many years of unquestioned speaking, requires patience and practice which the Spirit has in abundance but which is so seldom imitated in the church.

The descent into darkness, the darkness of a suffering, neglected and unheard people, is frightening for any priest or bishop. It may prove, at least in the short term, impossible or futile. Yet that is the divine model as enacted in Jesus Christ, a divine model born of years of experience of failure with God's first people. Last of all he sent his own son. 'This is the heir, let us kill him.' Not only the seed of the word, but the divine sower himself had to fall into the ground and die to bring new life. And Genesis, not Jesus, was the beginning. The rhythm of darkness, death and new life, of the darkness of the womb and the pains of birth, marks the story of creation as well as that of redemption. Over the millennia of creation and evolution, the Spirit remained patiently within the darkness of matter seeking ever more creative form, until co-creators could join her in the hazardous enterprise of human history. The patience of the Spirit had still to be tested by the waywardness of humanity to the point of surrender on the cross at Calvary. The test and surrender continue, sacramentally in the eucharist, more crudely and painfully in daily failure and suffering. Following the Spirit means following the pain-lines to join the powerless in the Spirit's creative and redemptive work.

Joining the powerless in solidarity, compassion or shared suffering, and then in resistance and transformation, summarises the divine involvement in human history. The recovery of that model of church is urgent in Ireland. The recovery depends, in human terms, on the discovery of the impotence of the present pretensions, spiritual, moral and intellectual. The moral and spiritual pretensions have begun to appear in all their impotence; the intellectual may need more attention. Irish society and the Irish church are not short of intelligent people. There is, however, little public interest in ideas compared to interest in literature and the arts. The church appears to lack serious interest in either ideas or the arts. Its intellectual weakness leaves it very vulnerable to ideologues, religious and secular. The debates of the 1980s on abortion and divorce exposed that weakness shamefully. The easy lurch into secularism in so many areas provides further evidence. Ordinary Christians do not have the intellectual training to face these challenges.

Christians with training (theologians) often do not have the freedom or the courage to discuss the issues fairly in public. Fear and frustration sap energy and compromise intellectual integrity to the point where the Irish church lacks any mental life of its own. This may be its most deep-seated weakness, rendering it unable to analyse its own needs and harness its own resources. Darkness of understanding in the Irish church is sometimes defended as loyalty or faith, as if God had created human minds but was unable to cope with their use. In the surrender to the Spirit, to which Irish Christians are now summoned, there may be a recovery of intellectual vigour, courage and integrity.

Recovery can only be by rediscovery of the true extent of the darkness and impoverishment, of the company of the impoverished and suffering, of the presence of the Spirit who first of all accompanies and so sustains. Beyond sustaining will come enlight-

enment and liberation when the surrender is stable and the company
is true.

First Steps

The stages of recovery, which involves a journey in darkness, are
not easy to chart. The first steps will be tentative and experimental.
So are the suggestions offered here. The whole company of Irish
disciples must be engaged in any recovery programme, and for this
a national synod or representative assembly will eventually be necessary. Just now, differing groups will have differing obligations of
differing urgency. For bishops and priests, the more urgent are
recognition of their own isolation and poverty, and of their need to
join these usually excluded by church and society: women as a general category, the socially deprived like the unemployed, the homeless and the travellers, and the religiously alienated.

Obvious opportunities for moving in this direction arise with
the appointment of new bishops and even new parish priests.
Instead of the usual display of ecclesiastical triumphalism at the
consecration of a new bishop, with rows of bishops and priests in
their finery, the occasion might be dominated by the local people,
with the conventionally last among them promoted to the front
pews. The new bishop and parish priest could spend their first
years listening to these last and least ones while they develop teams
and a strategy to explore the darkness with their own people. There
are already examples from which to learn, such as the attempt in
one diocese to establish a dialogue between bishop, priests and
women's groups. Such dialogue needs to be open and sustained
beyond the inevitable pain-barriers. There are many other excluded,
alienated, angry and indifferent individuals and groups requiring
attention and with whom learning should begin. Admission to
these groups is not automatic, and pain, even humiliation, will be
part of the price.

Priorities

The learning together process could cover the whole range of church
teaching. It may eventually need to. Meantime, priorities should be
established. These may vary from diocese to diocese, even from
parish to parish. Some co-ordination will be necessary within dioceses
and at a national level. This would clearly apply to the ever-delicate
areas of sexual morality and marriage where lay, and particularly
women's, insights are so badly needed. National discussion is clearly

necessary in discussing the relations between church and state, morality and law. These relations are changing in Ireland, but the church's contribution remains static. The same need and paralysis appear to characterise inter-church relations. The potential peace dividend for the churches has hardly been considered. Poverty and exclusion may operate more variably, but local churches and the national church need to engage with the poor and excluded them-selves, in fresh dialogue, analysis and reform.

Liturgical renewal, in face of declining Mass attendance, of the end of confessional practice for so many, and a much reduced num-ber of priests, has to begin at what Bishop Finnegan recently described as the 'rock-face' of the local church. A simple introduc-tion of seasonal penance rites with general absolution would be a useful beginning. More thought and prayer and experimentation by the whole Irish church will be needed to get beyond beginnings.

It is the need for thought that is worrying. Irish church energy is more available for any other activity. Without a serious commit-ment to scholarship and hard-headed intellectual analysis and debate, the church will remain captive to superficial diagnosis of its crisis and to shallow, quick-fix solutions. Like other institutions, the church might consider establishing a national 'think-tank' with the resources and freedom to explore the true dimensions of the crisis and develop long-term strategies. In any event, a much more open intellectual and theological life is a top priority for the church in Ireland.

The acceptance of the growing darkness, the discovery of one another and of the Spirit within it, could restore the sense of vibrant togetherness so evidently lacking in the Irish church, and indeed in the wider Irish society. It will be a slow and painful process. The renunciations involved will not come easy. Just now, the Irish faith-ful have a great need for what Karl Rahner has called 'faith in a wintry time'. The winter name of church can only be metanoia, repentance, a radical change of human minds and hearts, of human structures and practices.

CHAPTER 4

And the stone was made flesh

July 1995

> *Hearts with one purpose alone*
> *Through summer and winter seem*
> *Enchanted to a stone ...*
> W. B. Yeats

Alma Mater or Hard Mother

Bare foster care was all she ever offered. 'Maynooth is a hard mother.' Proud boast or lame excuse was never clear to students trapped in childish breach of rule. The rule, self-contained and self-justifying, was old law not new commandment. Its complex Pugin traceries were inscribed in tablets of frozen stone. It was the word made stone, crushing the tantalising fragile flesh. Of course Maynooth's stony-faced life of the 1940s and 1950s and for decades earlier had powerful antecedents in seminaries and universities across centuries and continents. That the harshness was not unique could be cold comfort to the frozen and the chilblained, the coughing and the occasionally tubercular. The military barracks regime had little tolerance for weaklings of any kind in its preparation of fighting members of the Irish Church militant for the unending war against the world, the flesh and the devil. It may have lacked the class or the pretensions of a Sandhurst, but it had the vision of officers and men serving worldwide in the Irish spiritual empire.

Diversions and Subversions

For all the severity of the regime, Maynooth students were never really short of strategies for survival. Their earlier inheritance, after all, was largely one of surviving, surviving penal laws or grasping landlords or simple poverty. College rules, even ones inscribed in stone, could not match their resourcefulness or finally suppress their humanity. The 'yah' and the 'sound man', the 'screw' and the 'bake', the 'gun' and the 'gunny' developed diverse and often devious ways of maintaining health and sanity. Mostly it wasn't easy.

Sometimes it proved impossible. Tragically that impossibility was sometimes discovered too late.

Survival was not dependent simply on student resourcefulness. Recreation had its structural and formal place. At least over the last century, ball-games were central to that structure. The spiritual empire was not won on the playing-fields of Maynooth but many a broken spirit was prevented or healed in vigorous sporting activity if sometimes at the cost of a broken leg. Inter-county stars in Gaelic football and hurling were often surprised by the toughness of inter-class games on the High Field. The summer championship games at home seemed much less demanding. They might have been better prepared by the viciousness of Junior House croquet. All human deviousness, malice and fun were there.

The games may have become too serious to be seriously subversive. Off the field and below the parapets the jokers, verbal and practical, were busy with mimicry and parody, with snares for the unwary fellow-student or staff-member. These gay subversives soothed many a troubled heart. Gallows humour at the Old Fourths' flame in the aftermath of a hyped-up Black Friday orders list could deflate the pompous and promoted, while consoling the rejected. Subversion of student solemnity about the self was always best done by students.

There were less obvious but more lasting subversions possible within the system itself. Text-book theology tended to indoctrinate rather than inspire. Lecturer and student could still encounter unexpected tongues of fire. Scripture, always potentially subversive, was usually constrained in unimaginative exegesis. Word and Spirit would occasionally fuse to set one singing on one's way past the enchanting stone. Other chinks and gaps appeared in the fortress of clerical orthodoxy as Homer or Chaucer, Aquinas or Einstein came filtering through.

The Prayer of Subversion

Prayer, studies and recreation formed the round of the day, of the week, of the centuries, all encased in solemn silence from dusk to, dawn with intermittent undertones of hilarity. The prayer could be like Eliot's history for servitude or freedom, for head and heart bowed permanently down, or for eyes reaching to horizons above and beyond all parapets and walls. This is the subversive thrust of prayer. The stone must yield to God encountering flesh, to flesh encountering God in neighbour, 'immediate', 'quasi'. The enfleshed

God does not offer stone but bread, daily bread, eucharistic bread. Yet that nourishing God could easily become tasteless and dehydrated, lifeless without the letting-go and the letting-come and the letting-be of the surrender, the surrender into the silence and the dark of the embracing mystery.

Too frequently the surrender was blocked. The would-be swimmer's fear prevented the letting-go, letting the waters bear one up. The silence turned choppy and menacing, the fresh waves too difficult to breast. With the instructor out of call, the surrounding deep seemed overwhelming. Suddenly and rarely, the threat subsided and the fear became promise. The swell of silence gently raised the mind and heart. There was a sweetness in the movement of limbs set free upon the waters. Gospel stories, images and icons were absent now, just the dark and deep embrace. This prayer of dark and silence, with all its subversive power, was too uncertain and too strange to be spoken of in a culture shy of God's strangeness. About prayer they were seldom helpful, the old Maynooth masters. Domesticated liturgies, tried and tired devotions, located meditations fitted more neatly into the frame of stone. Yet the regular and the liturgical never quite lost their capacity to provoke and subvert: with the 'Hail Mary' breaching the silence of eternity, the Magnificat overturning the seats of the powerful, and the re-enactment of Calvary rending the veil of the Temple and exploding the tombstones of death. The ritual words and actions were always on the verge of breaking through the stone barriers and tipping one over into the silence and subversion of the waiting God.

What role the prayer of silence played in adult priestly lives, it is impossible to say. The lonely stones of parish-house may echo with prayer-rich silence or with no more than the silent screams of pain at the cutting of the links and the absence of the God. 'They never taught us at Maynooth,' the easy scapegoating comment. On praying into the dark and beyond, the reticence for some was lethal. In a new century, the silence will be harder to hear and harder to bear. All will be speaking to all as they surface on the Internet. Will there be space and time for silence and darkness, for mystery waiting to become flesh? The visions and revisions of liturgical renewal seemed to stop just short of encountering the mystery. Persistent silent prayer could help restore that power and presence. Who will turn off the muzak?

From 'Syllabus or Errors' to 'Gaudium Et Spes'

The fortress church, with its stone ramparts of precise teaching and Latin liturgy and with its granite doctors of divinity, enjoyed (if that be the word) its most powerful period from the 1860s to the 1960s. Two crucial documents date and frame the period decisively. The first was Pius IX's rejection of the modern world in the *Syllabus of Errors* (1864); the second was Vatican II's acceptance of the (more) modern world in *Gaudium et Spes* (1965). This was inevitably the most stable, stone-bound period of Maynooth's life. The pre-1860s and the post-1960s Maynooths seemed to have been more transitional at times traumatic places echoing the wider church and society. Maynooth's 'stable century' had its own difficulties and dissenters, its own adventurous initiators. Walter McDonald and John Blowick may serve as symbols of the different. Consolidation, with clear ecclesiastical and financial limits, was paramount.

Flesh and blood were never eliminated but cold stone prevailed. Maynooth lacked any welcoming air. To outsiders it seemed, and was, inhospitable. Family visitors were so confined in time and space that many never bothered to come. Intellectual hospitality was little better, despite the development of the journals and the dual university status. For the students, debates, private and public, magazines, unofficial and official, dramatic and music societies helped breach the fortress. Strategies of survival and growth kept them alert to a wider world.

Rolling Back the Stone

Buried beneath the weight of commentary and debate, completed before most contemporary students of theology were born and before most teachers of theology today began their studies, Vatican II has become an historical rather than an historic event. Thirty years later, it is difficult to recall and to recreate the excitement of its convening and its concluding. But there was no doubt that the stone had been rolled back. The stone age was over. The petrified church had become flesh and blood once more. Women and men disciples were encountering a risen Body of Christ in a world no longer rejected or condemned but rediscovered as creation and new creation, sacrament of a new heaven and a new earth.

The gates of fortress Maynooth were also blown open. The ideals and ideas of a new generation of pastors, missionaries and theologians were replacing the stone inscriptions of Noldin and Van Noort. The clerical walls came tumbling down. Eager lay-students crowded the corridors and lecture-halls so long reserved to soutaned austerity. The cheerful, warm voices and colourful clothes of women and girls, staff and students, might be expected to melt any remaining hearts of stone.

The rush to resurrection in Maynooth as elsewhere was palpable, exciting and premature. The stone had been rolled back but the risen people of God proved as fractious and disputatious as Peter and Paul and countless predecessors. Set free from the bonds of centuries, they were intoxicated and confused. Leaders, many with little insight into what had happened at the council, were often fearful and ill at ease.

The publication of *Humanae Vitae* in 1968 was symbol and source of the fear and confusion. It revealed and reinforced incipient divisions about the how and what of the post-Vatican II church. And while the excitement and energy around a range of renewal causes, from liturgy to liberation theology to human rights, continued, the disillusionment had begun. The stones were reappearing as obstacles or missiles or fresh protecting walls, depending on your point of view. The more intimately involved, priests, religious and laity, bore the brunt of the new suffering. Many departed in search of greater freedom and creativity or out of sheer combat-fatigue. Vocations dropped sharply. Internal church disputes, theological and ideological, personal and political, became more destructive. Maynooth was no exception. The seventies and the eighties were different and painful decades. The pain is not over yet for church or college.

The Easter Garden and the Sorrow Garden

The Easter Garden of Jesus and Mary Magdalen was sacramental, a sign and realisation of the presence of the risen Christ. This presence could not be grasped and held. *Noli me tangere.* The disciples at Emmaus recognised him in the breaking of bread and he vanished from their sight. To Peter on the lake-shore he spoke of the death by which Peter should die. Christ had risen and would be with his disciples always but the human pains of living and dying could not be evaded. As he had so often indicated, anybody who would be his follower must take up the cross. The Easter Garden would provide the reassuring presence in faith, hope and love. The Sorrow Garden offered the pains of life and death, the shameful neglect of the sleeping disciples, the sharp wound of betrayal, the cry of near desperation, 'Let this chalice pass'.

The rush to resurrection had bypassed the way of the cross. The experience in the Easter Garden after Vatican II had ignored the continuing existence of the Sorrow Garden. The sudden appearance of so many hearts of flesh had overlooked the enchanting power of the stone. Maynooth's striking bicentenary garden, with its death-like stones and life-giving fountain, offers another symbolic guide to the human journey from sinful garden to garden of paradise. The co-existence of the Easter Garden and the Sorrow Garden for Maynooth, as for all of humanity, may be read in the rocks and lights, the waters and plants of this new Maynooth garden.

Already and Not Yet: The New Maynooth

Gardens are seasonal, with
    'a time for every matter under heaven:
    a time to be born, and a time to die;
    a time to plant and a time to pluck up what is planted;
    a time to kill and a time to heal;
    a time to break down, and a time to build up;
    a time to weep, and a time to laugh;
    a time to mourn, and a time to dance;
    a time to cast away stones, and a time to gather stones together'
    (Ecc 3:1-5)
The seasons are becoming harder to distinguish. Frost and snow in May 1995 – a bicentenary omen? Omen or accident, the climatic confusions are further reminders of the human and the Christian. The intermingling of the Easter Garden and the Sorrow Garden, of winter and summer, of spring and autumn, is a permanent feature of the Reign of God as manifest in Christ. Already and not yet. Already achieved, present among and within us but not yet come, not yet tangible or visible. Christians cannot control or determine it. They can only pray and co-operate in trust. Faith without seeing and touching the wound in his side, and the chalice still to drink. Bicentenaries are human constructions, worthy of joyous human celebration. Divine initiatives have their own timing.

We do know that the return of the stones, the recurring recall to the Sorrow Garden, does not exclude the Easter experience. It prepares for it. The preparation may be long and arduous but the angel of comfort will appear. The stone will be rolled back again and again. The stone has become the flesh and blood which now both suffers and rejoices. Tears of sorrow and of joy are definitive proof. Maynooth and the church may laugh and cry as they had not for a

long time. Christmas and Calvary coincide in the divine timing as
Eliot's Becket recognised in his Christmas sermon:

> For whenever Mass is said, we re-enact the Passion and Death of
> Our Lord; and on this Christmas Day we do this in celebration of
> his birth … For who in the world will both mourn and rejoice at
> the same time? For either joy will be overborne by mourning, or
> mourning will be cast out by joy; so it is only in these, our
> Christian mysteries, that we can rejoice and mourn for the same
> reason.

CHAPTER 5

The priest, the poet and the woman

An Irish Yearbook, Autumn 1994 – Autumn 1995

Time-Form

Period picking, essential to historians, is an exercise in imagination. Setting time limits on the flux of life, personal or social, involves imagining a series of alternatives and choosing between them. Good history like good fiction requires creativity in content and form. What is on offer here is neither history nor fiction. Its creative demands are comparatively insignificant; the choices of time and form prompted by personal preoccupation rather than national pressure. Yet the events and themes are of much greater import than their limited discussion here may suggest.

One further apologetic note must be struck. In many ways Ireland in the period chosen has been dominated by the 'peace-process'. The ceasefires called by the paramilitaries, Provisional IRA and Loyalist, at the beginning of Autumn 1994 and still holding, have absorbed much of Irish political, cultural and religious energy over the year. They figure only indirectly here; others much more expert in the origins, conduct and prospects of the *Pax Hibernica* should be consulted. In the background to the events and themes of this essay lie the challenges of peace and reconciliation in Ireland, a duo which have eluded the Irish imagination for far too long.

The Fall of the House of Niger

Cucullus non facit monachum. The cowl does not make the monk. The Irish religious tradition, with its penitential and bawdy dimensions, as well as the Irish literary tradition, was well aware of this salutary truth. Yet the age-old stories of clerical failure and the recurrent outbreaks of anti-clericalism in Irish history and writing had left most Irish people unprepared for the scandals of the last year. Paedophilia by Irish priests, even if proportionately few, has deeply shaken Irish church and society. The revelation by a television programme in October 1994 that a particular priest had been engaged in such practices for over thirty years, that his superiors had ignored or covered this up, and that the Attorney General's office in Dublin had held up for seven months his extradition to Northern Ireland to face charges, seriously undermined the authority of church and state. The government fell in a complex set of consequences. Bishops, priests and other religious could not of course be removed in the same way. The credibility and trust they have enjoyed so widely and for so long in Ireland have been critically undermined. Confusion within the Irish Catholic Church has been compounded by failures among the leaders to respond effectively and by the continuous drip of further sexual and related scandals.

The priest at the centre of all this has been Father Brendan Smyth, a seventy-three year old monk of the Norbertine Fathers at Kilnacrott Abbey, County Cavan. In many ways, his is the name of the year in the context of this yearbook. Not that there have not been other priests facing similar charges. Not that there have not been other highly publicised cases of priestly failure quite different from that of paedophilia. And not indeed that the failure by church authorities generally has not in some ways been more scandalous to the faithful. Brendan Smyth should not be isolated and made a scapegoat by bishops or clergy or even laity. He has, however, become a symbol of the collapse of the Roman Catholic episcopal-clerical fortress which seemed so unshakeable in Ireland almost since the days of the Famine, one hundred and fifty years ago. the black-suited brigade, with its military discipline and authoritative, and often authoritarian voice, has been humiliated. The House of Niger has fallen.

The roots of this fall are too many and too long and twisted in history to be adequately examined here. In hindsight, the eighties proved a bad decade for the Catholic Church in Ireland. The high point of the first papal visit to Ireland, in Autumn 1979, turned out to be just that, a high point … The enthusiasm and celebration, genuine at the time, did not lead to the renewal of the Irish church so badly needed. Instead it encouraged a triumphalist return to old ways and ideas already hopelessly inadequate to a radically changed and changing Ireland. The apparent success of these ways and ideas in the referenda on abortion and divorce in 1983 and 1986 had serious rebound effects. Many committed Catholics saw the 1983 initiative on abortion (mainly lay), and the conduct of some church people during both referenda, as manipulative and unfair.

The Catholic bishops and others seemed to have surrendered to a caucus which took a very negative view of developments in Irish society and a very literalist view of traditional Catholic teaching both on moral issues and on the relation between morality and law. The distinctions which Augustine and Aquinas had insisted on and their illumination by Vatican II in the *Constitution on the Church in the Modern World* and in the *Declaration on Religious Liberty* were simply brushed aside.

There is a strong case for describing this failure by the Catholic Church leaders as a failure of imagination. Many critics of the church, both loyal and dissident, would regard the Irish Catholic Church as singularly unimaginative. Further evidence for this attitude will appear in the later sections of this essay. It must, however, be remembered that for all its limitations the Irish Catholic Church in pastoral, educational and missionary initiatives had remarkable imaginative power in the previous one hundred and fifty years. Indeed the clerical failures of recent decades were still accompanied by imaginative justice commitments from the church at home and abroad. *Trócaire* (Mercy) and other church-inspired organisations committed to the developing world have been accompanied in their success by pastoral letters and practical engagements with injustice and poverty at home. The failures to anticipate and then to analyse the current clerical difficulties, combined with the continuing failure to offer an inspiring vision for the future, will continue to haunt the Irish Catholic Church as failure of imagination. That the Roman authorities display at least equal imaginative impotence does not excuse Irish church leaders at this critical time. For Rome, imperial and ecclesial, Ireland has always been marginal. For the Irish Catholic Church, marginalisation is a fresh experience. It could well be the source of renewal, but not if it is denied or railed against as somebody else's fault, that of the media or the intellectuals or the simply selfish.

Irish poets learn their trade
W. B. Yeats's famous admonition to Irish poets to learn their trade might be said by now, Autumn 1995, to have been taken seriously. The award of the Nobel Prize for Literature to Seamus Heaney is by far the most important symbol of that. The first Irish poet since Yeats to receive the award, the other two Irish laureates, Shaw and Beckett, were dramatists. Heaney is critically perceived in Ireland and throughout the literary world as a fine and careful craftsman as

well as an original and creative artist. The Irish nation and its literary leaders rejoiced in recognition of Heaney's personal achievement which has been immense. In yearbook terms, he is clearly the
poet. Perhaps even more than at the time of Yeats and that literary
revival, the recognition of Heaney honours an Irish world of poetry
rare if not unique in a rich history. In both languages, Irish and
English, Irish men and women poets are producing poetry of a
remarkable quality, as Heaney would be the first to recognise.
Kinsella, Longley, Mahon, and Durkin among the men, together
with Máire Mac an tSaoi, Nuala Ní Dhomhnaill, Medbh
McGuckian, Eavan Boland and Paula Meehan among the women,
continue to develop and enrich the tradition of Yeats and
Merriman, Ó Ríordáin and Ó Rathaille in a line reaching back to the
early Irish nature poets. The poet has returned to the centre of Irish
life, including Irish spiritual life, in a way many a priest might envy.

As Heaney may not be isolated among his peers just because of
the Nobel award, so poetry should not be isolated from its sisters in
literature. Irish playwrights like Brian Friel, Tom Murphy, Frank
McGuinness, Sebastian Barry and Marina Carr, as well as novelists
like John McGahern, William Trevor and John Banville, have
extended the Irish canon well beyond Wilde, Synge, O Casey,
Shaw, Beckett and Joyce. The psychic and spiritual energy which
animates contemporary Ireland owes much to the new literary
renaissance in drama and novel as well as in poetry. The artistic
renaissance is not just literary. Music, traditional, classical and popular, in adaptation, composition and performance, is enjoying a
vibrant life, as are sculpture and painting. More obvious in world
impact is the development of distinctive Irish films, with Oscar-
winning directors like Jim Sheridan and Neil Jordan.

The lists are easy and might be easily different and include other
poets and artists. The texts and themes are difficult. In his *Redress of
Poetry* (1995) Seamus Heaney has a chapter on 'Frontiers of Writing'
with special reference to the cultural frontier between Ireland's
Ireland and Britain's Ireland. Here, as elsewhere in the work of
Heaney and other Irish writers, background becomes foreground,
the threat and now the possible gift of diverse Irish traditions give
sinew and muscle to the writing and analysis. The quincunx, the
five towers of Irish imagination which Heaney invokes, could draw
together the resourceful but often hostile traditions. In the deepen-
ing and stabilising of the 'peace-process', the imaginative break-
throughs of Heaney and his peers will surely be of great signifi-

cance. The redress of poetry may be the most effective alternative to the conventional resort to arms, as 'a violence from within that protects us from a violence from without' (Wallace Stevens). At least it may 'help to hold in a single thought reality and justice' (W. B. Yeats, *A Vision*).

Here for good

The debate about the political and ethical nature of poetry, of much interest to Heaney in his recent book, takes a fresh and freshly Irish turn with the publication of Eavan Boland's *Object Lessons* also in 1995. Her sub-title 'The Life of the Woman and the Poet in Our Time' suggests the ethical dilemma in which she found herself, how to be an Irish poet and a woman. 'The majority of Irish male poets depended on women as motifs in their poetry,' she writes. 'They moved easily, deftly, as if by right among images of women in which I did not believe and of which I could not approve.' (p 134) 'All good poetry depends on an ethical relation between imagination and image. Images are not ornaments; they are truths' (152). The advent of Irish women poets has not just added to the tradition; it has changed it. Women for so long simply objects of poems have become authors of them. Women's experience in finding poetic expression has changed the poetic enterprise, at least in Ireland. Boland is well aware that this is not simply a parochial matter. Poetry everywhere is involved. She is also aware that it cannot be simply a matter of poetry or the arts. Life, society, politics are changed. In her poetry and criticism she has contributed with other women writers to this change in Ireland, perhaps the greatest single change in our society in recent decades. Where the priest and the poet, in different ways and at different times, might have seemed central figures in Irish society, and the women, by Boland's own assessment, marginal, a radical change has occurred in principle and in practice.

In 1995, as in the years since her election in November 1990, President Mary Robinson has been the symbol of this change and its inevitable frontiers-woman. Women in Ireland and all over the world see in her a triumph not just for women but for all the excluded and marginalised. She has changed politics more deeply than the woman poets have changed poetry. This derives from the happy coincidence of the curious office of the Irish presidency, where the power is primarily moral, the growth of women's public consciousness and skills, in which she played a notable role, the particular needs of Ireland at this time, and her own personal gifts. The impoverishment of the image of Irish women, which Eavan Boland deplores in the tired identification of nation and the symbolic Cathleen Ní Houlihan or Dark Rosaleen, may be halted in the face of a woman of flesh and blood, of heart and head, who embodies the Irish people so effectively just now.

The Heaney phrase 'Here for good' has all the 'two-mindedness' of the best Irish phrase. The permanence suggested may be combined with the ethical value to recognise the real achievement of the women's movement in Ireland. It has been basically an ethical movement for justice and freedom and goodness. If the renaissance in poetry and the arts might be described as moving from aesthetics to ethics, from beauty to goodness, from fundamentally self-delighting creativity to redress, the women's movement might be described as moving from ethics to aesthetics, from justice and goodness to beauty, from objects in poetry or society to subjects and authors. With the development of women politicians and women poets, and with the acceptance by some men politicians and some men poets of the feminine in themselves, the distinctions are not so neat while still illuminating.

A Triad on Trial

As the discussion developed in these last paragraphs about ethics and aesthetics, the usual third partner of religion was ignored. The title and structure of the essay as a whole demand some address of this partner despite recent humiliating events. Father Brendan Smyth and others do not fairly represent Irish religion but they remind it of its current or looming marginal status. For many people, it has been replaced as source of spiritual and moral energy by the arts, and justice movements like the women's movements. Yet in many of its historic forms, as well as in its Irish Catholic form, religion has interacted closely and fruitfully with art and morality. Indeed some of the greatest art works and most powerful moral movements have originated within, or at least been heavily influenced by, Catholic Christianity. Today in Ireland at least Catholic Christianity may have to adopt a much humbler stance as it seeks dialogue with artists and women, as it seeks in the name of religion to join the traditional triad of aesthetics, ethics and religion. The fundamentalist temptation to flee these worlds of artist and woman (*justitia* as well as *femina*) must be vigorously resisted. Only in dialogue and interaction with the moral and the artistic, as they flourish today, can the religious hope to renew religion. As Eavan Boland notes in her analysis of women and women poets, the margin may be the very best place from which to understand a society. For followers of Jesus Christ this ought to have great resonance.

Transcendence at the Margins

> And he came to Nazareth where he had been brought up; and he went to the synagogue and he stood up to read and there was given to him the book of the prophet Isaiah. He opened the book and found the place where it was written,
> 'The Spirit of the Lord is upon me,
> because he has anointed me to preach good news to the poor.
> He has sent me to proclaim release to the captives
> and recovering of sight to the blind,
> to set at liberty those who are oppressed,
> to proclaim the acceptable year of the Lord.'
> And he began to say to them, 'Today this scripture has been fulfilled in your hearing' (Lk 4:16-21).

Jesus invokes that other prophet and poet, Isaiah, to manifest his mission to the marginalised. The scope of that mission, as revealed in his ministry and teaching, reaches its almost inevitable climax in his death as a criminal outside the city limits. For Catholic Christians in Ireland, and particularly for their bishops and clergy, their being pushed to the margins may be providential. At least it will enable them to join Jesus' people of first choice. Many Irish clergy and religious have already taken this option, particularly with the poor of developing countries. The home-based might follow in greater numbers before they are finally pushed there anyway. From these marginal situations have come the most vital intellectual and pastoral renewal in the universal church, through liberation theology and its activists, women's theology, black theology, ecotheology and all the spiritual and pastoral energy which they have expressed and released.

These renewal activities are evident in Ireland also. 1995 marked the first and highly successful conference in Ireland on the ordination of women in the Catholic Church. The attendance and discussion confirmed the huge support which the BASIC (Brothers and Sisters in Christ) Movement had already received in its signatures campaign and the results of successive polls reporting a majority of Irish Catholics in favour of women's ordination. The publication of the Papers of the Conference this autumn, 'Women – Sharing Fully in the Ministry of Christ', is an important sign of hope from the margins.

Of course there are many other issues at the margin for women and others which a community of Jesus' disciples must address. However, it is in this location that they are likely to see them most clearly and pursue them most effectively. It is on the margins, not at the centre of human power, that they can bear witness most effectively to the transcendence which the search for justice, freedom and peace both illuminates and finally needs.

Truth and beauty are no less important marginal issues. Their entrapment in human power-structures has the usual corrupting consequences. The freedom of the artist is essential to her answerability. The beauty of her making is her way to truth. That truth and beauty signal transcendence for many. In the incarnate model of Christian faith and its sacramental expression, matter and language combine with human creativity to give a glimpse of the ultimate mystery of creating. Christian believers and leaders need to learn from creative artists that making and the delight in it comes first and only then judging or criticising and knowing (W. H. Auden).

A church leadership at the margins could help bring that difficult triad together again. The priest may join the poet and the woman in transforming Irish society. 1994-1995 may have seen the beginnings of that.

CHAPTER 6

Bruised reeds and the mystery of the church

October 1995

Father Tommy Waldron was buried in April sunshine in the burial plot for priests at Claremorris parish church. Only clergy and immediate family were allowed inside the railings. He would have been embarrassed by this further barrier, although aware of the limitations of space and appreciative of the large number of priests who attended. As teacher and preacher, however, as pastor and counsellor, his many strengths derived from being with and listening to the people, the students, parishioners and friends he loved and served. They made him the outstanding human being, Christian priest, he became. His church, 'the church he would like to wake up to' in the title of his last proposed article, was a church in which the baptised had the first places and the ordained were their faithful servants, gillies of God's people.

The Clash of Croziers

In the oppressive summer heat, the sound of croziers clashing could have been that of the first round in the episcopal All-Ireland. All a summer game for the hungry media, shortly to be eclipsed by Sonia as world champion and Clare winning the hurling title. Bishops clashing, as distinct from bishop-bashing, is unlikely to become a major sport. Yet the spat between Cardinal Daly and Bishop Comiskey, with its supporting programme, may be important in liberating the Irish bishops and the Irish church to address the deeper challenges facing them. Celibacy or marriage for the clergy is a significant issue which has become more urgently in need of debate recently. In the context of the church's real mission, it is a secondary issue, as some bishops recognised. Such recognition has its own ambiguities which illustrate the difficulties of many church and indeed broader debates. To describe celibacy as a secondary issue is to many people to suggest that it is unimportant. It is a strategy of evasion. To describe it as primary is to many others to lose a sense of proportion about the meaning and mission of the Christian gospel. Such emphasis may also paradoxically make the celibacy debate more difficult to conduct and resolve. Accommodation becomes less easy the more significant the issue appears.

The majority of Irish people, the vast majority according to the *Irish Times* poll, thought the primary issue was freedom of speech and of debate in the church. This is not without its ambiguities either. Which issues are to be debated and how? Celibacy for the clergy or eucharistic presence? In the popular media or in church fora? How are they to be finally resolved? By papal fiat? By episcopal majority? By popular vote of the people of God or their representatives? By the Roman Catholic Church or the church of all Christians? The questions could go on, accompanied by charges of evasion for raising them or of naïveté for ignoring them.

As the issues become more sensitive the positions become more polarised and the prospects of resolution more remote. 'What kind of church are we to have in Ireland?' emerged as a further gloss on 'the freedom debate' motion. This could embrace any number of issues. To address it would require a carefully prepared, fully representative and properly conducted synod of the church. Bishop Michael Murphy's endorsement of such a synod to deal with 'emerging divisions in the Irish church' received massive support in the same poll in the *Irish Times*. It will yield no quick results at home and perhaps none at all in Rome. Lessons, positive and negative, are to be learned from the Dutch and African synods as well as from the Pastoral Council of the Catholic Church in England and Wales. At home the annual meetings of the Church of Ireland, of the Presbyterian and Methodist Churches, could have much to teach the Catholic Church as it begins to experiment with representative and deliberative assemblies.

The Roman connection poses problems not just for a possible synod but, more critically and immediately here, and in the wider church, in the appointment of bishops. The lack of effective consultation and the imposition of very conservative bishops, sometimes against the express wishes of local bishops, priests and people, have created serious difficulties for a fragile church in places as disparate as Vienna and San Salvador. The exercise of Roman primacy in its contemporary style needs to be reconsidered, not just by the Irish church, but by the Roman Catholic Church throughout the world; and not just by Roman Catholics but by all Christian churches, if the Petrine ministry is to be offered, as it should be, to the whole apostolic community of Christians.

What kind of issue is this, primary or secondary? To formulate the question in regard to Rome's primacy may seem to some already schismatic if not heretical. Ambiguities abound, with many difficulties of both style and substance. How far can they be distinguished without putting at risk the validity of the Petrine ministry and not just the manner of its exercise? Historically, this ministry has been understood and exercised in a variety of ways. Present and past ways are not the only possibilities open to the Spirit and the church. A personalised and centralised papacy, with its combination of direct monarchial rule and curial bureaucracy, is not necessarily the final stage of a complex evolution. The Irish church has its own contribution to make to further development of the papacy. To ensure that, Irish disciples and their leaders will have to show more courage in fidelity than has been evident recently.

The Language of Mystery

'When you speak of church,' the first questioner asked, 'do you mean the bishops or the building?' 'Neither' was the truthful reply, followed by an attempt to explain its more fundamental meanings as people of God and mystery of God's presence. The explanation got lost *per ignotius*. Mystery is a sign and a warning sign of the unknown, unknown to the speaker as well as the listener. Recourse to the language of mystery is the last refuge of the baffled, detective, crossword puzzle addict, natural scientist, theologian. It presents too often as a cover for ignorance. In some religious situations it may be an arrogant cover for such ignorance and an obvious move to protect power. Speaking of the church as mystery sometimes sounds like yielding to such temptations. 'No questions please, it is a mystery.'

All religious language is inherently fractured as it seeks to encompass the unencompassable. For contemporary, even Irish audiences, fragmented is more apt than fractured. The fragments recur as sound-bytes in a myriad other discourses. The adoption of originally religious language in commerce or politics is a commonplace. There can hardly be a commercial company without its frequently revised 'mission' statement. Yet language, with pregnant words like love and justice and community, like mystery and God, is the only instrument available to discover and discuss humanity's deepest questions.

Recovering the Sense of Mystery

In Jewish and Christian tradition, mystery denotes the grand design of God for creation and humanity as it is revealed in the history of Israel and of Jesus Christ. Paul, the great New Testament theologian of mystery focused on Jesus Christ as central mediator of this divine mystery, without denying the revelation of the one true God to Israel, the Athenians' sense of God (Acts 17), or the revealing role of the things that are made in creation (Rom 2). Paul is characteristic of the whole tradition in developing his understanding of the mystery of God's presence and activity by moving between explicitly religious awareness, language or events and the awareness, language and events of the wider world.

In seeking to recover the sense of mystery today the same strategy may be useful. In a more explicitly religious culture, the beauties of nature as manifesting the glory and mystery of God could be taken for granted by psalmist and Isaiah, by early Irish poets and a host of medievals. Even modern poets, through Hopkins and Eliot to Patrick Kavanagh and Denis Devlin, still had access to the vocabulary and the audience for directly religious poetry. Indirection and ambiguity are more typical of today. Isaiah's bruised reed which shall not be broken (Is 42:3) may be a more promising starting point than Hopkins's windhover 'upon the rein of a wimpling wing/in his ecstasy'.

The present recovery in respect for nature and particularly for this planet began in fear at the dangers to the earth of human destructiveness. Bruised reeds were turning into the annihilation of many plant and other living species. Their destruction would eventually accomplish human destruction. Ecocide could only lead to homicide. Fearful for themselves, humans had to look again at their need to respect and conserve things natural, the non-living like air and water as well as the living. Fear for self and nature fostered respect and, beyond that, recognition and regard for these realities in themselves and not just as potentially useful or harmful to humans. In themselves and in their integral participation in a marvellously complex and intricate eco-system, the things that are found in nature display a dignity and a beauty that exploitative humanity had overlooked. Their foundness, their givenness, their beauty, not even Solomon in all his glory arrayed as one of these (Mt 6), their openness to further human understanding and fuller human appreciation, and their vulnerability to continuing human destruction: all alert us to mystery. In Christian terms, they are the gift of a benevolent and inexhaustible creator-redeemer who has called humans to be co-creators, but must continually double as redeemer in face of human tendencies to destroy rather than cherish, conserve and create. In this recovery of a sense of nature in its fragile dignity, and of a sense of humanity in its ambiguity, the way may be opened to some recognition of God's plan of creation and salvation, of Paul's sense of mystery.

The human reaction to a damaged ecology has recurring parallels in reaction to damaged people. In sudden emergencies caused by natural disasters or human failure or both, outsiders become suddenly awakened to the needs and dignity of victims of earthquake or famine or war. Historically the systematic oppression of people prompted the identification and promotion of human rights through international and national conventions and laws. Discrimination and exclusion based on skin-colour, ethnic difference, gender or poverty have nourished, in opposition, the sense of worth and dignity of each individual person and of particular peoples. Without the hurt, the dignity might never have been so effectively identified, protected and promoted. It is a dignity shared by all, found in all and not based on personal achievement or government grant. Its original foundness and givenness establish its inviolability, its transcendence of merely biological, historical or social construction. In principle, each is a world in herself, freely given, to be recognised and cherished by every other. Admission to that world is by invitation only. Only the self may reveal it. The sense of mystery returns. Without it, dignity and rights of the weak will not survive the intrusions and manipulations of the powerful. Dignity is highlighted in weakness. Bruised reeds restore a sense of mystery.

The human tendency to attack the weak, natural and human, did not confine itself to creatures. The darkest deed dared the inner sanctum of God in the show trial and execution of Jesus. In the vulnerability and death of God the Christian mystery in its full Pauline sense confronts us. Reflection on the dignity and beauty of earth or humanity as revealed in their hurt can prepare for this extraordinary *crux fidei*, without naturally satisfying us. The light cast by Calvary on human suffering and dignity is also important. The final affirmation of the dignity of humanity and nature is revealed in the Risen Jesus. He comes always by way of the cross, so our affirmation in dignity may not finally escape that route. This encounter with mystery in all its divine, human and natural dimensions, provides a lifetime's task for the prayerful, thoughtful and active Christian.

The Church: Presence and Proclaimer of the Mystery

The opening chapter of Vatican II's Dogmatic Constitution on the Church, *Lumen Gentium* (The Light of Humanity), is entitled 'The Mystery of the Church'. Pauline themes of mystery and its early Latin equivalent in sacrament are much in evidence. The community of disciples established by Christ to continue his work of announcing the good news of the reign or presence of God in saving power, is seen itself as a witness to and embodiment of that divine presence in power. It is seen as the Body of Christ, the New Israel, the Spirit-led people of God. In all this, it is to be a sign and realisation of the unity in transformation of all humanity.

Much of the language of Paul and John, so favoured in this first chapter, stresses the inner connection between the community of disciples and the Risen Christ. Baptism and eucharist are the critical enactments of this unity, or even identity, as disciples become members of the Body of Christ. They are buried with him in baptism to rise to new life, his new life. At eucharist they eat and drink the Body and Blood of Christ, become more fully members of Christ and so of one another. This awesome view of church and Christian remains central to understanding the church as mystery and to the church's mission to proclaim and promote the mystery of Christ and of God. As indicated earlier, it is not easily understood even by committed Catholics. Perhaps better, it is not always fruitfully understood because it is not critically understood or examined. The temptation to allow mystery prevent reflection is not always resisted by believers. So mystery degenerates into mystification with inflated claims and resistance to criticism. The hierarchical structure of the church may sometimes facilitate this, with the true mystery of Christ's presence obscured by human aspirations and arrogance.

Darkness Visible and **Lumen Gentium**

The bruised reeds approach to mystery has its advantage in discussing the church also. Given suffering servant and Calvary connections, it could hardly be otherwise. The distance established by the descriptions of the church as the community of disciples or People of God as compared with that of the Body of Christ, allows for cooler reflection. Disciples are followers of Christ and, if the New Testament is anything to go by, always a mixed bag. God's first people, Israel, offered a similar human mix in its history as a chosen and revealing people. The humanity and individuality of disciples and people cannot aspire to the human perfection of Jesus as revealing the mystery of God. Half-light may be more characteristic of the church of disciples than full sunlight. The 'light of the world' cannot simply dissolve human opaqueness.

At times, the half-light may give way to sunlight. At other times, it will succumb to increasing darkness. Human sin, personal and institutional, has always afflicted church members and leaders. It has affected attitudes, structures and practices in a history that we try to avoid studying and in a present that we may defensively misrepresent. The evidence is all about us. Yet these bruised reeds, these damaged people, betoken another level of mystery. They may make the human darkness visible in ways in which people with no claims to the truth and love of Christ may not. *O felix culpa.* No excuses may be offered. No plea bargaining, as if my sin was committed to enhance witness to God's grace.

The descent into darkness which a broken Christian or church may experience, involves personal or institutional failure. But to accept the descent, never easy but perhaps easier for person than for institution, is to accept the brokenness. It is to touch the bottom, as AA puts it. And the bottom is dark and threatening. One's very last inclination may be to let go, to surrender. The spectacle of a proud man letting go, still worse of a proud institution. And without letting go, acknowledging one's forsakenness, there may be no answering mystery, no ultimate salvation. For Christians, the answering mystery is God the Father of Jesus Christ. Both faced the supreme test on Calvary when darkness overcame the earth. Has Christ's church members and leaders who can face that darkness of Calvary and so restore the light to the peoples, the *gentes*? Of course it has. But who are they? And how are they to be discovered and released?

Repentance and Renewal

The mystery of the church takes precedence over the structures. Yet they are not separable. The debates about structures and all the other practical issues lead into the mystery. The sense of mystery makes sense ultimately of the structures. Reform of the structures is demanded in service of the mystery. Reform and renewal are initiated by the acceptance of failure and descent into darkness just outlined. They form the way into the kingdom through repentance.

The repentance (*metanoia*), by radical transformation of human minds and hearts, of human structures and practices to which Christians are continually summoned, applies in a particularly urgent way to the community of Irish Christians or church today. The first step in repentance is acknowledgement of failure. That is only slowly emerging from leaders of the Catholic Church in Ireland despite the recent leads given by Pope John Paul II in his acknowledgement of the church's failure in regard to women, and by Archbishop Eames in regard to the failures by the church of Ireland during the Famine, and indeed by Cardinal Daly in his address at Canterbury Cathedral. The Catholic bishops' reluctance may be partly because they see themselves under siege from the media, partly because of the persistence of an older defensive posture and partly because, as Kevin Myers pointed out in a purely secular context recently, institutions such as governments are very reluctant to confess failure by the institution. Yet the personal modesty and indeed humility of many church leaders must be seen to translate into institutional humility in open admission of mistakes and failures if repentance and renewal are truly to begin. The humbler church suggested in the wake of some spectacular failures in the past is overdue.

Such acknowledgement is, however, only the first step in repentance. And it will need to be more than verbal. It will have to demonstrate in deed, in a whole series of deeds, in a 'process', to adopt the in-word, that church leaders accept that they cannot overcome these failures by themselves. The Spirit of God in the church must be more actively attended to as the basic and finally inexhaustible source of repentance and renewal. Active and effective attendance to the Spirit in the church requires searching out and listening to the Spirit as it moves through all members of the church. Arrogant confinement of the Spirit to the church's episcopal leadership must pay the price of all arrogance. Renunciation of institutional arrogance is the Spirit's first requirement in the process of repentance and renewal. Led by the Spirit and in search of the Spirit, bishops will turn to priests and people. In line with the divine strategy operative from exodus to Calvary, the Spirit finds its most obvious home in the excluded and oppressed. To these, church leaders should turn firstly and persistently. But the Spirit is the Spirit of the Body of Christ, of the whole people of God. Allowing the Spirit to speak through them requires systematic and long-term conversation and co-operation between all members of the church. The rest of this article considers some practical suggestions on how to develop and sustain that conversation and co-operation.

Instruments of Renewal

It would be another exercise in arrogance to presume that such conversation or co-operation did not occur already, officially and unofficially. Bishops and priests with one another and with lay-people have their meetings and discussions, although the systematic character of these, their openness, and particularly their impact on the church at large, seem very inadequate to the present situation. There are quite a number of purely lay initiatives also, from Pobal and Basic at the national level to a whole range of local groups. An interesting sample of these was given in John O'Brien's valuable book, *Seeds of a New Church* published last year.

Surveys and polls are another element in the promotion of internal conversation in the church, even when they are conducted independently of any church auspices, as most of them are. Their limitations relate to their instant reaction style of information which does not issue from any serious discussion and may be unduly biased by the kind of question proposed. A different kind of initiative by lobbies collecting signatures for a particular position is also a value, but does not involve real debate among the signatories either. The recent Austrian referendum among Catholics may be a valuable emergency exercise but not a sufficient basis for longer-term renewal.

Without ignoring the value of any or all of these information, discussion and lobbying exercises, the Irish church should consider more comprehensive and public initiatives in seeking to understand and respond in the Spirit to its current challenges. The most obvious of these has been advocated for some time but, as mentioned above, most recently and influentially by Bishop Michael Murphy of Cork. That is a national synod for the church in Ireland. If there is to be a full examination by the church of its difficulties and resources, it is hard to see any real alternative to a synod. Its capacity to renew the church may not be taken for granted. Unless it is fully open and representative of the whole church, unless it is very carefully prepared, and unless it is implemented effectively, it could do more harm than good.

Careful preparation, a first essential, takes time. If the Irish Bishops' Conference should reach a decision very soon on calling a synod, and if preparations were to begin immediately, three years would be the minimum preparatory time. So the decision needs to be reached quickly. And it should not be reached by the bishops acting on their own in the secrecy of their conference. In the first stages, the Conference of Religious in Ireland should be involved. Representatives of the other main churches should be on the planning body, at least in a consultative capacity. The future of all Irish Christians is at stake now and not just that of one.

Three years is a long time for many hurt and impatient Catholics. The pre-synod period could be longer still and no absolute guarantee of relief and renewal then. Parallel to the synod's preparation, but independently of it, there is room and need for other initiatives. They could, of course, contribute to the preparation and work of the synod but would not be tied to these. Two possibilities are raised briefly here.

One of the more imaginative and effective consultations which occurred in Northern Ireland recently was that of the Opsahl Commission. In the opinion of many, it gave a critical voice to people unheard for so long and played a notable role in mutual education between the communities, a task still far from completion. It has been suggested that something similar could be initiated for the churches in Ireland. A small group of commissioners, dominantly lay and headed by some prestigious chairperson, could offer a unique service to the Catholic and other churches in Ireland over the next couple of years. Sponsored by some responsible body, and with the agreement of at least some bishops and church leaders, it could hold hearings in a number of places about what people expect from the churches in the coming years. With careful organisation, this commission's record of the hearings and final report should offer information and insights on the churches which might never otherwise be available.

The last suggestion is prompted by the vigorous cultural and intellectual life which this country enjoys at present. Very little of it seems to matter to the churches and the churches seem to matter very little to it. This seems harmful to the churches and out of line with both their older tradition and, for Catholics, with the thrust of Vatican II. A quite humble approach is needed here as elsewhere as the church seeks to learn from the cultural and artistic, intellectual and scholarly activity of Irish painters and poets, scholars and thinkers. To enable this, some group or review or centre may have to make a start. Why not an ecumenical centre for faith and culture sponsored by some university or religious institution?

When a Just Man Dies

After that dismal winter of the church, it was almost as if we needed somebody to die for us; somebody just, somebody clearly of the church but untarnished by the recent scandals and failures. In his final painful months, Tommy Waldron maintained his concern for the church. 'All I need now,' he wrote, no longer able to speak, just days before he died, 'is three pages along with what I have in my head and the article will be ready.' What he had in his heart was even more important. He died as he lived in trust, in his family and friends, in his church, in Mary and Jesus, in his summer God. It seemed much too soon, still so much to offer. It seemed much too harsh, to be incapacitated in his greatest gift, his golden speech. When the just man dies he goes before us to send the Spirit which will lead us into further truth. Tommy followed his Master in that. Eavan Boland – he would have liked the woman and poet parallel – says in her recent prose collection, *Object Lessons*, she would like a poem to grow old in. Tommy, like to many of his generation, would have liked a church to grow old in. It has not happened yet. It is really a desire for the eschaton, the final kingdom. Tommy made it easier for a lot of people to grow old in the only church we have and the church which his spirit and the Holy Spirit will help to renew.

CHAPTER 7

A church vulnerable to life and love

February 1996

The long slow climb of the lament for Irish Catholicism may not have yet reached its climax. Lamentation is a Jewish and Irish speciality, sometimes too easily invoked or excessively indulged. In this instance no, or at least, not yet. And to dismiss or curtail *caoineadh na hEaglaise in Éirinn* would be to insult those people who have suffered so much at the hands of their own church over the years and to betray a serious lack of appreciation of their pain and loss. The proper limits to a period of community mourning are not predictable. Further loss is not only possible but probable. Yet uninterrupted or unmodified mournings and lamentation have a self-destructive effect. In personal and family loss, the mourning is balanced by new life and love, sometimes quite literally when the death of a parent/grandparent occurs about the same time as the birth of a child/grandchild. In the mourning community of the Irish church, consolation and joy will return with the discovery and cherishing of new life and love.

A Community of Life and Love
At heart the church is constituted by the life and love of the Spirit of Christ. The public institution does not wear its heart on its soutane sleeve. The human face of God manifest in Jesus Christ is not always discernible in the official face of the church. Love and life, with all their untidiness and even disorder, can appear too threatening to those who see themselves responsible for the good order of the church. They are not likely to be the first people in the church to discover and cherish new life and love, still less likely to create it. Of course the conventional leaders such as bishops and clergy do not have exclusive responsibility for new life and love in the church. The primary author of all that is the Spirit; the co-authors are all baptised and believing Christians, the community church. Today the Spirit is calling the whole Irish community church to move through its necessary lamentation to a new phase of life and love. In

61

many small ways that move has already begun. In many ways it was never interrupted as a range of Catholics, lay and clerical, got on with the Lord's business of life and love in the midst of distress and disintegration. Christ is with his church in these grim times as at all times, although he is not so readily recognisable.

The new life and love which the Irish church needs in such abundance just now, will take many forms and emerge from many different sources by the most various routes. Alertness to this variety and the skills to discern it and its source, the Holy Spirit, will have to be developed in the church. Creativity itself will have to be recognised and valued as a God-given instrument of new life and love. The programmes of prayer, consultation and experimentation which all this may involve, and the mistakes that may occur *en route*, are truly daunting although no more so than any purely human enterprise of creativity and transformation. Having a family is the most immediately concrete parallel. To bring children into the world is the most audacious and risk-laden human enterprise imaginable. Establishing or radically reforming political societies carries enormous risks. The creative work of scientists is full of risk for themselves and, as this century testifies, for humanity as a whole. Poets and artists risk exposing themselves in endless painful ways as they follow their creative vocations.

For the Christian, all this human risk-taking for the sake of love and life, in a spirit of creation, has its originating source and ultimate guarantee in the divine risk-taking of creation and redemption. The particular cost incurred need not be laboured here. What is significant is the intrinsic character of such risk-taking to creative-redemptive activity, divine and human, ecclesial and familial, political, scientific and artistic. In the context of risk and of the pain and loss which it may involve, the phrase 'vulnerable to love and life' seems apt. The invulnerable never suffer the pain but they can never enjoy the love or life either. Recent events in the church exposed a certain vulnerability among its clerical leaders. How that can be translated into vulnerability to love and life is an immediate challenge to them and to the whole church.

In exploring the challenge, this article concentrates on three rather artificial groups: women in the church; theologians; clergy, particularly bishops. The groups are described as artificial for different reasons. Internally among themselves they may differ very deeply. Externally, in the context of the church, they are closely related to and dependent on other groups and on one another.

Finally, other groupings could be suggested, such as lay or religious, which are at least as distinctive and as mixed. They have at least as large a role to play in responding to the challenge of a church vulnerable to life and love. The choice of these three groups is no doubt influenced by personal factors. The more objective justification can only emerge in the discussion of each group.

The Great Absence

The great absence from official leadership of the church for almost two millennia has been that of women. That alone would be sufficient justification for turning to their experience and insight in seeking to understand the present serious crisis. If the experience and insight of male leaders proves inadequate, as it seems to, then the logical alternative is that of women. The church is not the only institution in which male insight is proving inadequate. In others, the absence of women is no longer so great and the presence is, in some notable cases in Ireland and elsewhere, effective and creative. Poet Eavan Boland has argued that the emergence of women as poets in Ireland has changed the nature of the Irish poem. At any rate, a church in difficulty with declining male resources of leadership cannot ignore the option of turning to women's experience, insight and energy for help.

Women already play critical roles in church as well as in society, through parenting, teaching and a range of caring activities. They have more direct impact on the religious formation of the young at home and in school than priests or bishops have. Religious educators in second level, as well as primary schools, are increasingly lay and female. At least two-thirds of the students taking theology or religious education at third-level institutions are women. Women, lay and religious, exercise a whole range of formal and informal ministries in the church. That experience and expertise is not, however, integrated into the policy and decision-making of a church which needs both very badly. These ministries of parenting, teaching, nursing and caring are ministries of direct exposure to the pains and joys of life and death. Here only the vulnerable are valuable.

By their historic exclusion and marginalisation, women have experienced another dimension of vulnerability. This they share in varying degrees with all the excluded and oppressed peoples of the world. Many Irish women would not be as excluded or deprived as some Irish men, such as travellers or the long-term unemployed. In the larger world, many men are excluded and oppressed for religious, racial, economic and other social reasons. Yet wherever men are oppressed there is another deeper level of oppression, composed of women and children. This applies around the world, from Irish travellers to Mexican Indians. The developing solidarity in suffering, which is emerging among women worldwide, offers some real hope of overcoming it. It also offers a challenge to male leaders in society and church to show their own solidarity and exercise their own influence and power to help liberate the oppressed.

Church leaders have a double responsibility here because of their call to follow Jesus in the work of liberating the oppressed and because of their responsibility for the centuries-long oppression of women within the church. Pope John Paul II's recent apology to women for their treatment by church leaders was a welcome but painful reminder of this. A church leadership seeking to be vulnerable to life and love could hardly make a better start than by humbly joining with women, not only in their vulnerability, but in their 'vulneration'.

There are many women's groups in Ireland where priests and bishops might start learning the deeper lesson of a Christianity vulnerable to life and love. Other groups will be necessary, established by women themselves or encouraged into existence in individual parishes or dioceses. They must be respected, listened to, learned from, and not manipulated as a front for clerical power. This will be a slow and painful process for women and clergy. Anger will erupt from time to healthy time. As a stage on the road to justice, anger is valuable. As a search for vengeance, it becomes destructive. In the present very painful situation for many women in the church, the skills of conversation and the grace of perseverance will be very necessary for women and clergy, including bishops. For them in particular it could prove a particularly painful schooling in vulnerability to love and life.

The Wound of Truth

The special responsibility of theologians in the church is to the truth. It can be a costly responsibility. Despite the overall commitment of the whole church to truth, its foundation in Jesus Christ who is the truth, and the guarantee of the Spirit's guidance, the church's history records many painful debates and divisions about truth. Central to these debates and divisions on all sides were theologians, people who had the ability, training and commitment to seek further understanding of Christ's truth in new circumstances and in face of new questions. Theologians' service to that truth may be mixed in its results at any particular time. (How did so many of them justify slavery for so long?) Yet, it is an essential service because of that double gift of God, the revelation in Jesus Christ which has to be understood, preached and lived in continually changing circumstances, and human reason which must continue to make sense of that revelation. Only theologians truly open to the life and love of the gospels, and to the living and loving possibilities of their time, can serve the gospel community faithfully. Once again, only the vulnerable are valuable.

It is no secret that Irish theologians, however vulnerable, have not been treated as particularly valuable in recent times. This is a pattern of behaviour in the church reaching far beyond Ireland. The distrust of theologians is not confined to bishops. Many priests and lay people regard them with suspicion. The church as a whole does not seem to cherish intellectual ability and integrity in maintaining the essential dialogue between revelation and reason, between faith and culture. Perhaps it was ever so. Intellectual giants of the past and present, from Origen to Aquinas to Newman to Rahner, have suffered official church hostility, so why should the pygmies complain? Only pygmies would complain about personal slights. For committed theologians, openness to the truth can easily lead to misunderstanding by themselves at first, and when that is overcome, to misunderstanding by others. In a community seriously concerned about truth, misunderstandings and controversies are inevitable. Theologians are called to endure these into loving resolution, which may not happen in their lifetime. Suffering comes with the theological territory. Vulnerability to truth involves risk and hurt. Although no particular risk or hurt guarantees the truth of the position espoused, the theologian who has never risked or been hurt for the sake of truth is not likely to have contributed much to understanding the gospel.

Personal hurt to any theologian, then, is not the real reason for regret at the neglect of theology in the Irish church. The lack of intellectual vigour and rigour at the centre of the official church's debates and decisions has weakened it in a rapidly-changing society. Of course theologians have to do their own work, however unrecognised and unvalued it may appear. Many Irish theologians have sought to do this although their work remains marginal in its influence. In such critical Irish issues as the relations between church and state, between law and morality , inter-church relations, sacramental development, faith and prayer in a secularising society, women in the church, the idolising of economics at home and abroad, Irish theologians have diligently been seeking fuller Catholic and Christian understanding. This has not always been an agreed understanding. Only the wider church provides the proper context for that. And on some issues, agreement may not be possible for a very long time. On others it may not be necessary. What is necessary is that the theological agreements and disagreements take the pressure of the whole believing community so that its faith and practice may be challenged and enriched. Then the positions of the theologians can be tested by the Spirit of the whole church.

Theologians, still mainly male and clerical in training, have to examine their own consciences. Lack of openness to a wider truth may easily affect those limited to a particular constituency. It is noticeable and humanly understandable that like-minded theologians congregate together. They attract like-minded audiences. They review and approve like-minded books. They dismiss the unlike-minded very easily. The small scale of Irish life and its natural sociability may sometimes balance that. At other times it simply obscures it. It is a particular responsibility of those theologians who expose openness to seek a more inclusive theological mind and community, even if it results in recurring rejection. Another test of theologians' vulnerability to truth in life and love.

The distrust or dismissal of theologians may not all be due to simple anti-intellectualism or fear of changing truth. Theologians may appear cut off from immediate demands of personal or parish life. They may use language remote from the concerns of ordinary believers. Their intellectual concerns may seem to have no bearing on the pressing needs of priests and people. Some of this may be true and justifiably true. The technical language of theology is sometimes necessary and not always readily translatable, although theologians may exaggerate the need for it outside the learned journal. Some intellectual concerns essential to the health of theology are not immediately relevant to every believer, although they may be of great interest to some. Issues of the relation between Hinduism and Christianity might not be relevant in Ballyhaunis although relations between Islam and Christianity would. Hindu-Christian relations are potentially of interest to all Christians because they raise critical questions about the salvific value of other religions, about the uniqueness of Jesus and Christianity, about the church's mission to preach the gospel to Hindus or Buddhists, Muslims or Jews, about relations in prayer and spirituality, about personal salvation outside the church and so on. Some of these are relevant in some form for every Irish believer and are coming in the Hindu form, if not immediately to Ballyhaunis then perhaps to Ballyconnell.

A criticism of Irish theologians more difficult to counter would be their lack of engagement with the pastoral and social issues of the day. Their time and energy are limited. Teaching and research make very difficult demands. Scholarly research and writing have been notoriously lacking in Irish theology. All this and more amount to a significant counter-argument against the allegation of absence from pastoral and social engagement. Yet if Irish theology is to be truly Irish but not isolationist, and truly vulnerable to Irish needs and possibilities but yet rigorous, its practitioners must cultivate deeper engagement with the life of the Irish church and of Irish society. Poverty and peace, poetry and prayer, might symbolise areas where Irish theology needs to dig deeper.

Theology is not the preserve of the professionals, necessary though they be. Developing a community of professional theologians, still a real need in Ireland, should be a stage on the way to developing a community a thoughtful and searching believers. A church vulnerable to life and love must also be a community vulnerable to truth, the truth which sets free but, in the process, is bound to hurt.

Creative witness or juridical power

The fears of bishops and clergy, that the church as a believing community will collapse without the strong assertion and reassertion of a teaching authority with juridical power, may not be lightly dismissed. However, the case that only such a juridical church authority will preserve the believing community has to face two serious questions: How far is the strong use of juridical power effective at present? How far does it reflect the authority which Jesus bestowed on his church? These are questions for much fuller debate than any one writer could tackle. It may be that discussion of the role of bishops and priests in the Irish crisis will be more helpful than more direct and necessarily much longer attempts to answer the two questions posed. They will no doubt persist, as the jargon has it, as subtext.

By concentrating earlier on women and theologians in seeking a

church vulnerable to life and love, a particular context has been set
for treating here partially of bishops and priests. To focus the issue
sharply, perhaps too sharply, this section is concerned with how
bishops and priests may learn from and with women theologians,
rather than how they may teach them. Learning with and even
learning from implies teaching, which is to be seen, for adult
Christians certainly, as a form of mutual enrichment.

Because of their exclusion from the adult and further education
of priests and bishops, and because of their particular experience of
vulnerability, women are given the primary role. How far will the
clergy be open to this? How far will they be able to let go of their
traditional authoritative position to enter fully the role of disciple?
Will they really believe that they have much or anything to learn
from a group of women in their own parish or diocese? Will they be
tempted to go along with the forms without sharing the substance?
Will it be *pro forma* listening or real communication and education?
Will they have the skills for all this or the patience to develop them?
And will the women have the skills and patience? Can the mutual
education continue in face of some apparently irreconcilable conflict, over women's ordination for example?

These and other difficulties will continue to arise and to breed
difference and anger with theologians as well as women. They will
truly test the openness of priests and bishops to the presence of the
Holy Spirit in the whole people of God, indeed test their real belief
in a people of God. Yet if they persevere in faith, hope and love,
they will begin to share in that vulnerability to life and love which
many Christians exemplify but which is so often lacking in the public face of the church.

Genuine learning together creates genuine community. Mutual
formation is community formation. For bishops and priests engaged
in this learning process, community bonds will be formed which
will sustain real authority. It will no longer be just the abstract
juridical power of *auctoritas* but the concrete creative witness of *auc-
tor*. What juridical authority is necessary, effective and compatible
with the New Testament, will more easily appear in a cloud of such
episcopal witnesses.

A vulnerable Church: A Frontier people

A church vulnerable to life and love is not just necessary for the survival of the church. From the New Testament to Vatican II, the
church has been called to be the sign and instrument of God's pres-

ence and power in transforming and fulfilling humanity, known as God's kingdom. The church, by its values, standards and practices, is called to provide a model and guidance for the good society. In so far as the church failed to practice these kingdom values itself (and it frequently did), it could not offer effective standards and guidance to society. Society's needs for standards and guidance are at least as great as ever they were. And what they need is example not exhortation, witness not rhetorical appeal to external authority. The church is called to be a kind of *avant garde* of the relations and structures which ought to protect and cherish all human beings. The baptised and believing people of God is to be a pioneering people, a people at the frontier of new relations for the whole created people of God. In answer to that divine call, it must needs be a people vulnerable to life and love.

CHAPTER 8

The 'christening man' and the priestly people

October 1996

A couple of weeks after her younger sister's baptism, the three-year-old triumphantly greeted the visiting priest: 'You're the christening man.' True enough and nice to be recognised by a smiling three-year-old; it could still provoke the difficult questions which haunt all his tribe. The identity and role of the priest in a church whose identity and role are undergoing serious revision is cause of much headache and heartache to Catholic priests the world over. In Ireland, it has assumed its own painful form and intensity.

Between demoralisation and complacency

Without rehearsing one more time the oft-discussed difficulties of priesthood and church, one recurring feature deserves notice. The latest serious public scandal of sexual abuse or authority abuse reinforces the demoralised condition created by previous scandals. The latest lull in the storm, or any slight positive turn in the church's fortunes, revives much of the old triumphalist complacency. With the disappearance temporarily of the negative symptoms, a cure is quite likely to be proclaimed and ecclesiastical business resumed as usual. 'The church always survives these crises.' Yes, but where, in which tradition and to what extent? In the North Africa of Cyprian and Augustine, in nineteenth or twentieth century industrialised Europe? The promise of Jesus to be with his church always, and the guarantee of the Spirit, do not relieve the church, its members and leaders, from seeking to understand and respond to the deeper sickness which afflicts it from time to time. Their failure to do so so often in the past frustrated the work of the Spirit and left a divided and disappearing church in much of the Northern hemisphere. The recurring temptations to complacency and to presumptuous appeals to the Spirit could do further and irreparable harm to the weakened church of the West and North.

Restoring Confidence through Confession and Conversion

Demoralisation is not the only or the proper alternative to complacency. The healthy rhythm of Christian and indeed human living moves from recognising illness and failure to acknowledging the need of help in fuller diagnosis and effective healing. True Christian confidence, as distinct from complacency, begins with confession of failure. It is born of the humiliation of Calvary. The process of conversion, to which confession in Christian terms leads, is always difficult and usually partial. Repentance is required again and again for the individual Christian. In the case of Christian community, the difficulties are greatly increased and the partial character of the achievement more obvious. Structures last longer and become more rigid than persons. In seeking the personal and structural conversion which the church now needs, rigidity and resistance are bound to obstruct. The inadequate follow-up in letter and spirit to Vatican II amply demonstrates that. Thirty years and a generation, even a civilisation, later, Vatican II itself no longer provides a blueprint for the conversion needed, although it can certainly provide inspiration and important guidelines. Its partial success in developing a fresh vision for the church, in itself and in its mission to the world, could help now in stimulating the confession and conversion necessary to renewed and authentic confidence in the Spirit of Christ. The council's failure to deal satisfactorily at the time with the identity and role of priests, is a useful reminder of the limitations of authoritative assemblies and documents in responding to critical questions.

'To Whom Shall We Go?'

 The crisis and the *kairos* of the present time will not be met simply by appeal to assemblies and documents, however authoritative. Although they will have their place, it will not be the first place. The first place is that of the Christ. In Peter's words (Jn 6) 'To whom (else) shall we go?' Only he has 'the words of eternal life'. Even the sketchiest knowledge of the Jesus of the gospels makes for difficulty in recognising him in the church of the day. By one of those ironies, attributable no doubt to the Spirit, the return to the Bible and the gospels promoted at Vatican II has rendered the present hierarchical church less credible to the more biblically educated among its flock. Many attentive readers of the gospels find the present exercise of government and ministry in the church completely out of tune with Jesus' behaviour and teaching as recorded in the New

Testament. Of course, they find much in the lives and teachings of individual bishops and priests which is admirable and even evangelical. What they do not find is a community of disciples into which bishops and priests and even pope are fully integrated in faith, hope and love as members of the one Christ. The hierarchical structured organisation, with its juridical values and practices, seems a far cry from the *koinonia* of Jesus or Paul's organic bodily metaphor for the community of disciples. Cutting through the current confusion and historical complexity, to the One who has the words of eternal life, is never easy but it must be attempted anew by every generation of disciples and priests. Only so can the identity of church and priests be rediscovered or reinvented.

Locating the Christ

'Where do you meet Christ in the eucharist now?' a priest asked theologian, Kevin McNamara, after a lecture at the Maynooth Union Summer School in the 1960s. Rehearsing recent teaching of the council, the theologian explained that of course you still meet him in the consecrated elements of the bread and wine, that you meet him in the priest, but that you also meet him in the Word as proclaimed and, finally, in the assembled community itself. Another theologian (James P. Mackey according to reports) was heard to whisper, 'The real problem is not where do you meet him, but how do you avoid him?' It was not entirely a humorous comment, certainly not an irreverent one, as it drew attention to the pervasive presence of the risen Jesus in his Father's world, at once enriching and demanding.

In turning and returning to Jesus Christ in conversion, a range of presences is on offer. They are not, of course, isolated from one another. Their deep and inner connection, despite their fragmentary appearances, rests on God's acceptance and glorification of the crucified Jesus, the incarnate divine one and the 'first born of creation'. So Jesus' presence in word and sacrament clearly relates to Jesus' presence in the community of believers, but also to Jesus' presence in the whole of humanity and in every human being, particularly the least ones; to Jesus' presence in creation as well as to Jesus' presence with the Creator. Conversion to Jesus means turning gradually and repeatedly, if often only partially, to these various realisations and manifestations of his presence. The christening man must, along with the rest of the believing community, develop the skills and practices of such continuing return. Avoidance of one particular manifestation of the presence, in gay or other marginalised people for example, affects the closely connected other presences. Such avoidance damages Christian faith as awareness of and conversion to the full range of Christ's presence. Renewal in confidence for the christening man will start from this integration with the believing community into conversion to Jesus the Christ.

Body of Christ and priestly people

Initiation into the Body of Christ through faith and baptism establishes basic Christian identity. Membership of Christ, adoption as sister or brother of the Son of God, cannot be replaced or improved upon in terms of Christian identity. Discussion about priestly identity must begin here. Priesthood is first of all and only, according to the affirmation of the Letter to the Hebrews, to be attributed to Jesus Christ, our one High Priest of the New Testament. The New Testament's further refusal to use the term priest (*hiereus, sacerdos*) at all for people with various ministries, while it applies the term in speaking of the priestly people in the First Letter of Peter and in Revelation, reiterates the need to seek a fresh understanding of ministerial priesthood in the priestliness of the people which forms the whole Christ. Whatever the ordained minister is and does derives from his membership of this priestly people. To rediscover his identity and renew his energy he must return to his people, this historically embodied presence of Christ. The absence of energy and initiative, the apathy and paralysis which can afflict individual priests or bishops or groups of them, is often due to their self-isolation from their people and so from Christ. In human terms, a large organisation like the church depends on the energy and creativity of its wider membership. The age profile of the present church leadership, and its traditional caste character, cuts the leadership off from the messiness and energy of community life. In Christian terms, it deprives them of immediate contact with the multiple expressions of the Spirit of Christ which his people as his Body provide.

Christian identity and energy may be located in the Christian people as the first discernible domain of Christ's Spirit. The tasks dominantly assigned to ordained priests and ministers, the tasks of presiding at the eucharist and the other sacraments, of preaching and of pastoral care, the tasks of the contemporary christening man, have to be more specifically shaped and performed from within the identity and energy of the priestly people.

Assuming, as most Catholic scholars do, that the first-century ministry was complex and even confused, stressing, for example, apostles, prophets and teachers, the emergence of bishops, presbyters and deacons at the beginning of the second century has set a more or less dominant pattern since. However, of none of these was *priest* used at this early stage. The one priesthood of Jesus Christ, and the need to differentiate from the Old Testament priesthood, would have prevented this. Later, in the third century, the presbyter began presiding at the eucharist on his own and much later, in medieval times, he became equivalently the massing man. By now the eucharist was understood in strongly sacrificial terms and ordination increasingly understood in relation to the eucharist (Aquinas, *et al*). With the inevitably restrictive reforms of Trent and the potentially open reforms of Vatican II, this minimal sketch of the history of ministry and priesthood indicates at once the strength of tradition and its variety and changeability. At the beginning of the second millennium, the clerical priesthood began to emerge. At the end, it is reaching the limit of its usefulness and is withering away. A new understanding and practice of ministry and priesthood, baptised and ordained, is necessary and, by the creative power of the Spirit, already on the way. The key factor in its emergence is the return to the priesthood, mission and ministry of Christ located in his priestly people.

Mission and Ministry

Jesus is the model of ministry and mission. Ministry and mission belong together inseparably in Christ and his church. As the Father sent (missioned) him so he sends his disciples. They shall serve (minister) as he has served. The mission and the ministry are to the whole world and for the salvation, healing, fulfilment of the whole world, not just the human world but all of creation. The Word, through whom the world was created, is to complete and perfect that work of creation. For all the human disruptions and the discontinuities of an evolving material world, the divine creative power reaches towards fulfilment in God's reign or kingdom. The announcement and promotion of the kingdom which Jesus inaugurated, he carries forward through his church and its ministers. That carrying forward is entrusted to all members of the church as members of Christ. All are called to be priest-ministers and missioners after the fashion and form of Christ. Christian identity and energy are Christ-shaped in the actions of service to God, to humanity and to the world.

Mission and Ministry of the 'Christening Man'

The leadership of the ordained minister, the priest, which historically developed into clerical separation, will find many opportunities for renewal in the contemporary search for reintegration into
the priestly people. The basic identity, energy and shape of the ministry is rooted once again in the community that is Christ. That
shape may be described in a variety of ways. Three elements
remain essential, the ministries of word, of sacrament and of pastoral care. In all these elements of ministry, the priest remains at the
service of the baptised community so that, for example, the whole
Christ may be offerer and victim in the symbolic eucharist enactment of the drama of saving the world. It is from within the community and with the community, in *persona Ecclesiae*, that the
ordained acts out the identity and energy of Christ, *in persona
Christi*. These two descriptions of the ordained and their functions
may not be opposed or even separated if the priesthood's radical
foundation in the community that is Christ is to be maintained. In
the following sections an attempt will be made to look afresh at the
three elements of ordained ministry against the background of the
christening man's return to the priestly people.

'Produced and directed by Rev P. V. O'Brien, CC'

Through many decades amateur drama societies provided useful
centres of community life in the cities, towns and villages of
Ireland. The establishment of competitive drama festivals, culmin-
ating in the Athlone All-Ireland Festival, both improved standards
and intensified community self-esteem and general well-being.
Many of these societies were founded or directed by a local priest.
One of the more successful of these priest-directors was the late
Pádraig (P. V.) O'Brien of Tuam.

Recalling this priestly involvement has multiple relevance here.
Irish priests had always a larger sense of their vocation than that of
the sacristy and the sacrament. They did and do see themselves as
engaged in helping to build local community in ways beyond the
strictly religious. They saw this in human terms as a valuable and
often necessary contribution to the survival or thriving of a particular historic community. Its deeper interpretation, as expressing and
developing the kingdom announced by Jesus, was seldom explicitly
stated but often instinctively recognised. While priests still play
such roles in invigorating community life, they have to be sensitive
to the cultural and social changes by which people rightly see them-

selves as taking the leading roles as producers and directors, not only in the drama society but in every local cultural and developmental group. The priest, in accordance with his interest and competence, may be encourager or advisor or even scene-shifter. All this will facilitate his own integration into the community, human and Christian. No longer Chair of the GAA club and without automatic access to an All-Ireland ticket, he will enjoy the team's triumphs and suffer their failures with the community as a whole.

Not only has the priest's role changed in community development. The primary areas of development and its primary agents have changed significantly also. Environmental protection groups, parent-teacher groups, parents against drugs, self-help employment groups, movements for peace in Northern Ireland at local and national level, are joined by Amnesty International and support groups for Children from Chernobyl and for human rights in East Timor. The initiators and agents in these new areas of community consciousness and community building are very different from those of the middle of this century. Many are much younger. Few are clerical or otherwise in established positions. A very high proportion are women, and not just in issues immediately affecting women and for a long time ignored by a dominantly male culture. In the broader community issues women, including many religious sisters, have been pioneers, organisers and sustainers in new and essential community work. Sr Stanislaus (Stan) Kennedy, ISC, might well in church terms replace Rev P. V. O'Brien, CC, as director and producer of a set of real rather than theatrical dramas. Of course women without the trappings of religious vows provide most of the leadership and without quite the hierarchical taint of even producer-director. Facilitators, enablers and empowerers form the newer categories of social ministry.

Directing the Performances of a Lifetime

All life is drama and all dramas are dramas of salvation. Mostly, both on and off stage, the drama is not very dramatic and the salvation is not very salvific. Yet from Brian Friel's *Molly Sweeney* through *Coronation Street* and into Main Street, Ballyhaunis, the struggle for survival or salvation, the low or high intensity war between good and evil in all its ambiguities, persist until death do them part. Deaths and births, loves flowering or betrayed, heroic achievements self-destructing, even nothing happening twice, Sam Beckett style, in many a lost and lonely life: all these involve the tension and release of life and drama. Their ultimate significance may be simply ignored. For religious people concerned with the ultimate in life, they may be interpreted in different ways. For Christians, they reflect something of the biblical drama of the Jews and of Jesus.

If, as Vatican II and many subsequent documents and commentators suggest, the first responsibility of the ordained minister is the proclamation of the good news in preaching and teaching, his basic text is the Bible to be interpreted and performed in life. The living word of God, as recorded in the scriptures and as interpreted and lived in the Christian community, provides text and stage directions. Of course, the ordained have never performed this role on their own. Initiation into Christian faith for the very young was the work of parents, or sometimes today of grandparents. Most teaching of scripture and doctrine in school has been the work of the baptised with or without religious vows. Nowadays, even the theological training of candidates for the priesthood in seminary or university is shared with theologians who are lay people or religious women. And the homily or sermon for the special occasion is often entrusted to some appropriate preacher outside the ranks of the ordained. This is a (theo)logical follow-on from the regular use of lay-readers of the scriptures at Mass.

Given his leadership responsibility and his special training, the priest operates as producer and director of the major presentations of the scriptures in the parish. The increasing familiarity of parishioners with the scriptures, which it is his duty to promote, will modify the role of director towards that of facilitator and enabler. Partnership in parish, in Enda Lyons's telling title, will require partnership in preaching as well as in teaching, and in the preparation and evaluation of both.

There are further and even deeper reasons for developing this partnership. Preaching and teaching are not simply about memorising and understanding the classical texts of scripture and of the Christian tradition. As the dramatic analogy suggested, the goal is not memorising and understanding the lines but performing them. Indeed, as any good director or actor might admit, the lines are only finally understood in performance. Priest and parishioners are performers all. Fresh understanding of the lines and relevant direction of performance are learned together as the production, the live production, proceeds. Fidelity to the text does not prevent, indeed it demands, innovations in production. This goes far beyond any creative attempt by a great director like Peter Brook to present a new version of *King Lear*, interesting and insightful as that might be. Brook is seeing new dimensions in the text as he places it in dialogue with the context of his time and draws on new and inventive actors and designers to uncover these dimensions. Interpretation and performance of the Christian texts is a task for the whole Christian community with all its diversities and ambiguities. And not for a neat core of professional actors. Christians are all and always amateur performers. Priests, religious, catechists and others may rightly value their professional skills in organisation, direction and presentation, but when it comes to Christian performance they remain amateurs, in that good sense of loving commitment and persistent inadequacy. Unreal expectations have compounded the scandal of recent public failures. For all that it demands of every baptised Christian, the performance of a lifetime, achievement is mixed and finally unavailable to human assessment.

Performative interpretation or understanding, and preaching the word of God by living it, is a community task. No one, ordained or not, can presume to do it for another. Only in interdependence on the living insights of all can the community begin to approach any satisfactory understanding. This becomes more evident as the dialogical nature of the scriptures themselves are recognised. Documents of living communities, their words of God were constantly mediating between the faith of the people of Israel and surrounding peoples and cultures. This was no less true of Jesus and the New Testament writers. In theological terms, this might be described as the necessary dialogue between the word of God in continuing revelation and the word of God in continuing creation. The dialogue between faith and culture, as it is sometimes described, is still essential and can be carried on effectively only by the believing community as a whole. It is primarily culture with a small c, the whole life, achievement, failure and aspiration of a community in its fuller context. Culture with a capital C, which can distil so much of the larger culture into the lines of a poem or the performance of a play, has a critical role in the dialogue, as P. V. O'Brien and colleagues knew very well. Preaching out of the community is the prelude to preaching *to* it. All the talents of the community prepare and enable both. In this preparation and enablement, the christening man retains a position of leadership and responsibility.

The wedding will take place in St Mary's Church, Westport

The sacramental or sanctifying responsibility of the priest is also an

enabling or facilitating one. One cannot make somebody else holy
or even ensure their true participation in the sacraments. This is
true of the central sacrament of the eucharist, where the priest has
for too long been seen to dominate. His role as facilitator and his
integration into the community may be more easily charted by
examining the great dialogical sacrament of marriage. The key dialogue is between bride and groom in their 'yes' to each other and in
the many preparatory yes's and no's, queries, answers and evasion,
certainties and ambiguities during the months or years beforehand.
In the best of cases, this protracted dialogue involves genuine
preparation in religious as well as personal terms for the life-unto-
death dialogue which is initiated on the wedding day. In preparation, remote and immediate, in organising and directing the cere-
mony, in ensuring continuing support in good times and in bad, the
christening man plays an important role. Although he is the official
church witness to the public dialogue of consent which constitutes
the sacrament, he is not the minister of the sacrament and his witness signals a community witness as well as a community commitment. Before, during and after the actual sacramental celebration of
marriage, the priest is called to prompt and if necessary co-ordinate
the care and the support which married couples and families so
often need today. At the clear and persistent service of the married,
personally, in pastoral teams, or through Accord and similar
resources, the priest become ever more integrated into the believing
community. He bears witness with that community to the pro-
foundest dialogue of all, that between creation, to which marriage
primarily belongs, and salvation, to which sacraments belong. In an
age where it is said that the sense of the sacred is often lacking, the
emergence of the delicate flower of human loving, its confirmation
in the steely commitment of 'I do', and its exuberant expression in
one flesh, enables the human and created to reveal the sacred and
transcendent. To this the priest and the whole Christian community
is called together to bear sensitive witness.

The first item on the agenda

The priest's return to sources within the priestly community is
made the more difficult and fearful by the divisions endemic to any
large and diverse community. These divisions may be religious.
The Catholic Church is quite divided at present at both the clerical
and lay level. Some of the divisions are deep and bitter. They may
be complicated by social divisions no less deep and bitter. How is

the priest to be integrated with people at odds over restructuring the sanctuary or managing the school or girl altar-servers or accommodation for travellers or accommodating with unionists ...? The first item on too many agendas is that split. Yet, among the christening man's chief responsibilities is reconciliation, social and sacramental. The social may be the more urgent. Indeed, without serious attempts at the social, the sacramental may finally disappear or, worse, become meaningless. Reconciliation is not achieved by standing apart. Only from within, with all the misunderstanding that will involve, can the christening man or any Christian hope to contribute to any reconciliation. A serious contribution will usually be a costly one. The reconciler is never far from the Calvary of Christ.

From collaboration through collegiality to community

Theological buzz words abound and confound. 'People of God' became a slogan without substance. 'Communion' seems likely to go the same way. 'Collaboration', 'collaborative or shared ministry' could suffer the same fate. Even 'praxis', the great answer to much theoretical theology, has become embalmed itself. Words cannot be dispensed with, but they should not be dispensed at all by Christians where they are not rooted in living practice. They must be working words. *Laborem exercens* should be the test. Hard labour together is what makes genuine colleagues and a genuine college, academic or ecclesial. The first step to collegiality is not verbal or theoretical, but practical. Through actual collaborative projects in the parish or diocese, in the national or international church, colleagues are formed and collegiality becomes a possibility. Colleagues who have worked in Accord or St Vincent de Paul or Trócaire develop a sense of equality and respect that is genuinely collegial. At parish and diocesan levels, many lay-clerical projects are urgently needed, from preparing liturgies and sermons to preparing people for sacraments, to tackling particular social problems. If the needs are real and the working together involves genuine equality and respect, colleagues are formed. This is even more urgent at diocesan and national levels between bishops, priests and laity. From a college of colleagues authentic community derives. What has been given by the Spirit in baptism takes human form in living community. Mere rhetoric gives way to a priestly people into which the ordained are gradually but truly integrated.

The return of the Christening Man

Three-year-olds don't forget. She still recognises the christening man on his return visits, but naturally is free from theological hang-ups about how far he belongs to a clerical caste and how far he is becoming a full member of the priestly people into which her younger sister was recently inducted. He can't escape that challenge so easily. The turn and return to the priestly people involves a continuous and painful process of conversion. Repentance is the more appropriate Christian term. At this stage in the development of the church in Ireland, a clergy, bishops and priests, leading the way in repentance would be a powerful sign of the continuing vitality of Irish Christianity. As in that great parable of repentance, that of the prodigal son, the clergy would also know the joy of being welcomed home by God among his people who are also their people.

The ministry and mission of the NCPI

The National Conference of the Priests of Ireland, to which all ordained priests in Ireland in theory belong, has clearly a responsibility to its own members, and to the wider church and society, in facing the current difficulties of Irish priests. By its very existence it symbolises a certain unity and mutual support; a collegiality of priests which transcends boundaries of parish, diocese and religious order. It relates positively, if still in very limited ways, to the Bishops' Conference. Priest-bishop collegiality has still a long way to go at diocesan but particularly at national level. For that and other reasons, the Conference of Priests has to develop more clearly a voice of its own in analysing the challenges to the church and in responding to them. Perhaps it is only with such a mature voice and a greater sense of solidarity that it will be ready for collegial dialogue with the Bishops' Conference.

The mutual support and care of priests for one another is more urgently needed today than ever. A National Conference can contribute to the recognition of this and to developing an attitude among priests themselves which would help them to enable one another. The cry of the spirit was very evident in some of the recent heartbreak cases involving priests, where the individual priest said he had nobody to turn to. Of course, more than a change of attitude is needed. Professional help as well as personal care must be available on terms actually acceptable to wounded priests. The NCPI could and should be concerned with developing these services.

The emphasis of this article, however, is on the integration of the ordained priest into the priestly people of the baptised faithful. In that community setting, priests will find their deepest support and affirmation. There they will help form the basic Christian *collegium* of service into which they can hope to draw more fully their episcopal colleagues. From that fuller community-college can come the imaginative initiatives in dialogue and collaboration which may overcome the present swing between panic and complacency. By locating the primary presence of Christ in the community, and turning to that Christ as source of identity and energy, the 'christening men' will themselves be renewed in faith, hope and love.

It is in that spirit that NCPI over recent years has been examining in detail the difficulties and resources of Irish priests. In that spirit, it has moved to set these difficulties and resources in the context of the priestly people, with new NCPI committees on Women and the Church, the Role of Theology, the Church and the Media, and the Church as Community. It is in the same spirit that it is seeking to develop its regional meetings to address broader issues of the church and to include a broader representation of the ordained and baptised. The Spring 96 consultation on *Challenges Facing the Irish Church* sprang from the same concerns. In its invitation to representatives of the church as a whole, including members of the Reformed churches, it sought with at least partial success to promote the integration of the priestly people. The Annual Conference, Sept 16–18, at St Patrick's College, Drumcondra, aimed to take the discussion further in theme and setting. The theme, *The Irish Church in Dialogue*, attempted to bring out the positive enterprises of the priestly people in Ireland without ignoring the difficulties. The setting stressed once more the need for integration between ordained and baptised.

Without daring to hope for too much, it may be that such an approach will transcend some of the more divisive issues around priesthood, from celibacy and the ordination of women to the more basic problem of the meaning of ordination. All may be seen in the clearer light of the Spirit, who will not finally be frustrated.

CHAPTER 9

Should the healing begin at Christmas

December 1992

Should the healing begin at Christmas there my be no rush of hidden hurt to stable door, disrupting devout shoppers on their pilgrim way to worship in temple at Macy's and Toys'R'us. We are not ready for the healing touch (not yet, O Lord), as we luxuriate in our hurt, relish the prospect of revenge on neighbour, lover, unionist or Serb. Just teach them a lesson; protect our rights; let them stew awhile; ensure a final solution or at least a decent apology. Not yet, O Lord, the healing that reeks too much of the sword in the scabbard, of turning the other cheek, of Father forgive them … and they know damn well what they are doing. And forgive us as we forgive them … forget it or ignore it or just pretend it.

Anyway the healing most people want for Christmas is more personal; from that disturbing report on the lymphatic gland, from the aftermath of heart by-pass or breast surgery, from AIDS developing in yet another parishioner, from depression recurring, from the painful breaking of a long and loving partnership, from the open wound of buried parents. Personal illness and loss give little time or energy for fresh communal tragedy in Yugoslavia or Somalia. Time, boredom and hopelessness anaesthetise against the routine ruptures between nationalist and unionist, Catholic and Protestant. No healing is sought or expected.

The slower, deeper fragmentation of Irish society, the anxieties of keeping up, leave little energy for attending to the sufferings of those being kept down as the middle fragments up and down. The fragmentation is not just economic. It is also geographical, educational, vocational, religious, cultural, social and political. The painful symptoms of 1992 – record unemployment, Miss 'X' and the Supreme Court, bitter election and referenda campaigns, the resignation of the Bishop of Galway – all may be relieved by forgetting or ignoring. Healing is another matter. Who wants healing when victory is possible? And when victory and defeat are by, will the victors not rest content and the defeated bide their time?

But should the healing begin at Christmas, at least the shepherds and the angels will rejoice. The marginalised and the idealists will sing glory and peace. The healing may be like biblical death, coming when and where one least expects it. For the healer is the God, the infant God and the crucified God. Only by enduring the wound of humanity could the God be a truly human healer. Birth and death, their dignity and indignity, enabled the God to insinuate the divine self into the most painful wounds of the human body and mind, into the most bitter hurt of the human heart. There is no human pain, physical, mental or social, where the God has not been, where the God is not still, where the healing is not ready to begin.

Abortion is always a tragedy. It can bring great pain, especially to mothers who have made the traumatic decision to have their babies aborted. That decision is often made in fear and loneliness, under very great pressure from the circumstances and from other people. It is often made with the most intense regret and reluctance.
(Irish Bishops' Conference, 5 November, 1992)

Should the healing begin at Christmas, the good news must get out not only for them, the mothers of such pain and their babies, but for all of us. There's only us, no them and us. (President-elect Clinton did well to pick this up in his nomination speech in an ugly election.) If one member suffers we all suffer. It must not have appeared like that to many of the women reluctantly compelled, as they saw it, to seek abortion. Bearing one another's burdens, in that other Pauline phrase, did not really extend to the burdens of motherhood, often abandoned motherhood, as the bishops also note. The provident innkeeper in all of us would not get involved. There was bound to be another inn or at least a stable down the road and a clinic just across the Irish Sea. We were losing contact with the hurt and the needy and so with the presence of the Spirit of healing. Contact can be restored. The healing Spirit is among us. Let that healing begin at Christmas.

Not only for mothers but for all women damaged by the crude contours of male dominance. Deeper social healing requires the liberating reconciliation of women and men. Sexism is a sin, according to a proposed pastoral by the US Catholic Bishops' Conference. As so often, it seems to be a sin of the others. We are not ready yet to acknowledge our part in the systematic exclusion and reduction of women. Should the healing begin at Christmas, reality and symbol may slowly change. With altar-girls taken for granted, participation by women in decision-making processes of the church would enrich its wisdom and mission and restore its sacramental role as healer in this painful area.

The church as sacrament, effective sign, of healing needs revitalisation and extension. The decline of the conventional practice of the sacrament of penance and the absence of developed alternatives have diminished the church's healing presence. A repentant and reconciling turn to women could be the public sign and sacrament that the healing does begin at Christmas. The list of others damaged or excluded by church or society is long and difficult. If a repentant and healing church is to give a lead, is to be a sacrament, it must face the task of integrating these, the unemployed and the poor, the homeless and the travellers, the sick and the elderly. There are some who can seem more painfully *other* still, like the homosexual. What healing integration shall the Christmas church bring them?

Should the healing begin at Christmas, how much will it have achieved by January's Church Unity Week? The Advent month and mood of repentance could be, for divided Christians, essential preparation for their healing celebration of their Lord's birth. They must express that turning to one another in symbolic or sacramental form. Otherwise they ignore the incarnate, sacramental strategy of God's healing presence and betray their own vocation to be Christ's sign of unity.

The arguments against these divided Christians sharing in the great sacrament of reconciliation and healing, the eucharist, are frequently repeated and theologically significant. (Some of them were used forty years ago to prevent Christians saying the Lord's Prayer together.) As the healing proceeds it may be time to reconsider admitting shared eucharist, at least on special occasions, to reflect the shared faith, hope and love already by the gift of God present, and to promote fuller unity. That fuller unity in difference Cardinal Ratzinger described in his address to the European bishops as 'reconciliation in diversity'. In the dynamic of healing, ways of celebrating, faithful to the tradition and acceptable to the churches, will be found. No doubt the shepherds and angels will be at hand with their glory and peace.

Should the healing begin at Christmas, the need for arguments will diminish. Only the Spirit will know to whom and when and for what reasons the healing has come. In the complexity and multiplicity of personal and family relationships, the most subtle analyst

or the most sophisticated computer could not predict the twists and
turns which may convert painful rejection into healing acceptance.
What is ultimately the work of the tracking and enabling Spirit
does, however, need to be enfleshed. Human attempts to describe
the enfleshment must needs be tentative, approximate, symbolic.
The scope for prosy description or lengthy analysis is very limited.
Only fragments and images may be possible.

The broken marital or personal relationship has its own peculiar
Christmas pain. The emotional glow of Christmas presents, or visiting children, can be misleading. Christmas healing will provide no
romantic ending to the pain of years. Yet it could initiate the healing
years of gradually recovering love.

> Should the healing begin at Christmas,
> Tight-lipped 'Fine' may give way to soft-voiced 'Hurt',
> fearful silence become fragile conversation,
> the Venetian glasses emerge from their angry box.

The first grieving Christmas blows cold and chill. The house
estranged subverts the urge to celebrate as 'they' would have wanted.
The generations close in to cover the gaping hole which can make
word and step so treacherous.

> Should the healing begin at Christmas,
> the grief turned outward to Jerusalem and its children,
> may see the horizon rolled back
> and observe the departed among the arrived.

The last lingering Christmas defies inhospitable death or shrinks
despairingly before night interminable. To have come all this way
for death midst the celebration of birth. How can one speak of healing in the absence of cure, in the presence of death?

> Should the healing begin at Christmas,
> without the hope of medical cure, just AZT,
> how will the wasting body accommodate
> the spirit's need to move beyond itself in love?

The hurt child that is parent of the hurt adult finds pain anew at
Christmas. Psychic wounds from events no longer remembered
restrict loving and accepting love.

> Should the healing begin at Christmas,
> the painful pain of infancy may finally unfold
> and the fugitive blob be tenderly reshaped
> to serene beauty by often unspoken loves.

The public hurt is also personal, sometimes devastatingly so. Ireland had its share of public hurt in 1992. There will always be need for healing of hurt done to and by the public. Plastering it over is no more than that. Yet to go beyond that requires a delicacy and precision that human skills and words seldom allow. And yet should Christmas speak,

Should the healing begin at Christmas
will seventy times seven extend to all
or must one exclude the obviously scandalous?
passionate bishop but not cold, unforgiving Christian?

Public and political pain are closely connected. Their range and call are planet-wide. On Ireland's nearest land-mass, some of the worst political pain of recent times runs its destructive way. Historically Christmas truces offer little hope of true peace but the voices of the shepherds and the angels may still be effective.

Should the healing begin at Christmas,
ethnic cleansing may abandon its Herodian ways,
Croat and Serb shed their armoured disguises
and join the naked infant in the human race.
...

Only fragments and images and fragments of images.

PART II

Fragments Communing

CHAPTER 10

Liturgy and Christian life

1. Introduction

(1) Meaning and purpose

In the important sense that liturgy is an essential constituent of Christian life, the duality supposed by the title of this article is misleading. As involving formal, communal and explicit activities of Christian worship, liturgy may be distinguished from the rest of Christian life. Distinction without separation is central to the Christian and Jewish traditions. The further complexities of the relationship, whereby Christian life is a form of worship and Christian worship a concentration and manifestation of the life, will gradually emerge. The purpose of this chapter is to expose and explore these complexities as they have developed in the Christian tradition and continue to challenge the Christian community.

(2) Liturgy and moral theology

As a central theological discipline, the study of liturgy is relatively new. In the Catholic tradition, moral theology has been a major, to many a dominant, part of theology since the Council of Trent. Although there was no adequate alternative for a time, it would be a mistake to call moral theology a theology of Christian life in that phase. It was too narrow in scope, too juridical in form and too preoccupied with the failures of sin. Its relationships with liturgy were extrinsic and legal. The obligation to attend Sunday Mass, and the requirements for validity and licitness in the sacraments were typical.

The renewal of moral theology, and its ambition to become a theology of Christian life, coincided by and large with the renewed interest in the liturgy and in its theological significance. Since Vatican II this has led to a more self-conscious interest by both moral theologians and liturgists in the interaction between worship and Christian action in the world. Eucharist and justice, a theme frequently addressed in contemporary theology, would have been unintelligible to moral theologians of an earlier generation.

These welcome developments raise a number of problems for theologians. How does one study moral theology, as theology of Christian life, in separation from liturgy and also in separation from doctrinal or dogmatic theology and scripture? Who can command the expertise to range over these disciplines and their historical evolution? Is some new alignment of specialities required? Should there be specialists in (provisional) synthesising as well as in analysing theological issues? Is team theology now necessary? What form could it take? It is necessary to mention these questions here to alert readers to the inevitably partial treatment of the relationship of liturgy and Christian life which is all that is possible here, not for reasons of space but for reasons of method and expertise in current theology.

(3) Outline

The main section of this chapter will involve systematic exposition of the Christian tradition and its current understanding of the relationship between liturgy and Christian life. The biblical and historical basis will be, for the most part, integrated into the systematic. This in turn will open up some new questions or rather new aspects of perennial questions. Theology shares the pilgrim condition of its people, God's people. In this area theology has still much exploring to do. As the people of God moves on, so do theological areas of exploration.

The emphasis will be on the interaction of formal Christian worship and general Christian living in the idiom of contemporary moral theology with all the attendant limitations. After a brief comment on the biblical and historical background (ii), the systematic sections will deal with (iii) Liturgy, life and the kingdom of God; (iv) Divine word and human communications; (v) Sacraments, society and environment; (vi) Kingdom values and sacramental engagement. More exploratory sections will consider (vii) the problem of evil, sin and redemption in terms of consumption and communion and (viii) the triune God and a holistic view of liturgy and life.

II. Biblical and historical background

A few biblical points need to be recalled and underlined. The Mosaic covenant, central to Hebrew religion, maintained a close

connection between response to Yahweh and response to the neighbour. Its charter in the decalogue is so structured. The great eighth-
century prophets, their predecessors and successors, insisted that
liturgical worship of God was futile, indeed offensive, from a people who neglected and exploited the poor and the stranger. Justice
(*sedaqah*) in life was essential to authenticity in liturgy. Love of God
and love of neighbour belonged together.

The relation between love of God and love of neighbour was re-
emphasised and deepened by Jesus and the New Testament. Prayer
without care was valueless. Indeed the New Testament reader
might be forgiven for taking love of neighbour as the only test of the
authentic follower of Jesus (Mt 25; Rom 13; 1 Cor 13, *et al*). Such a
life of love does, however, depend on love for God and particularly
love by God, who first of all loved us (1 Jn 4). This love by God was
manifest above all in Jesus' death and resurrection, recalled and
shared in the liturgies of eucharist and baptism (1 Cor 12; Rom 6).

The basic connection between liturgy and life shaped the early
church. Christian life was that of a member of Christ's body into
which Christians were integrated in baptism and by which they
were nourished in eucharist. Serious life-failures (sins) cut people
off from such sharing unless they repented and were forgiven in the
liturgy of penance. Christian moralists, subtle and sophisticated
like Clement of Alexandria, or harsh and prophetic like John
Chrysostom, maintained the crucial connection between true worship and good living. Liturgy as summons to, judgement on and
empowerment of Christian life remained a church constant through
the centuries.

III. Liturgy, life and the kingdom of God

The early Christian linking of Christian liturgy and Christian life
emphasised, without always developing, the intrinsic nature of
these links. Yet the incorporation into Christ by baptism, the nour-
ishment in eucharist, the reconciliation in penance, shaped from
within the new life of the Christian, its liturgical actions and its life-
tasks. The seven sacraments were themselves related to critical
needs and moments in Christian living and dying. The word of
scripture carried its saving power and significance as part of every
complete liturgy. In seeking an integrating vision for the celebration of liturgy and the challenge and achievements of life,
Christians are bound to look to the kingdom of God preached and
inaugurated by Jesus. Despite its linguistic awkwardness in many

modern contexts, God's kingdom remains the most comprehensive and fertile symbol for the new pattern of worship and living established by God for humanity through Jesus Christ.

This kingdom, in its 'already' stage, is to be discerned and celebrated. In its 'not yet' stage, it is to be prayed for, striven for and received. Christian liturgy, in its remembering for the future, symbolises, realises in word and sign the divine achievement of the kingdom in Jesus and prays for, anticipates its complete human and cosmic reception. Humanity and cosmos are opened to the healing and transforming presence and power of God by the community of disciples, taking bread and wine as Jesus' body and blood until he comes again. What is announced in word and signified in sacrament liberates human beings and cosmic forces to seek the fullness which is to be theirs by the self-giving of God. Human and cosmic fulfilment, by the transforming presence and power of God, is the scope of the kingdom as symbolised in the liturgy and expressed in the Christian living of the explicit and implicit followers of Jesus Christ.

IV. Divine word and human communications

The conventional duo of word and sacrament, with their Reformed and Catholic-Orthodox associations, can be useful in more detailed relating of liturgy and Christian life. Their essential belonging together must not be ignored if artificial divisions are not to emerge in Christian community and life as well as liturgy. In undertaking in this section then, to examine in detail the relation between word of God and human communications, the word-sacrament unity as proclaiming and realising God's kingdom must be kept continuously in mind. Human communications in turn are not to be understood in a narrowly verbal way but as meaningful expressions between members of the human community which are in turn forming (or deforming) of that community.

Liturgy as word of God and human language communications share many of the great dualities of the human condition. Both are received (as gift) and achieved by human effort. For the word of God, gift and reception may be the more obvious aspect. Yet the decline of any single dictation theory of inspiration, and the increasing awareness of the human construct and the human struggle which shaped the diverse documents of the Hebrew and Christian scriptures, reveal the other dimension of the Bible as word of God, human achievement. The role of the word of God in liturgy requires further human effort from presenter and listener if the gift is to be effectively received.

Human communication is clearly a matter of some human effort and achievement. Yet each receives the language of parents and larger community as a gift. The struggle to speak, to communicate, is the struggle to learn a language which has been handed on as tradition and gift. Even the great refiners of language in literature are operating out of gift, of a language given, of talents received, of people encountered and not invented, of experiences undergone, often without any advance planning, and certainly without predetermined conclusions.

The word of God and of humanity as gift to be recognised and accepted, celebrated and enjoyed, marks a critical connection between liturgy and Christian life. An ethics of speech and communication for Christians will start from this divine and human gift to be celebrated, in part by celebrating the donors. Praising God in liturgy, and honouring one's father and mother and community in the language received, draw together the liturgical and ethical. So did the decalogue in the range of its ethical demands and in the original liturgical setting of its recitation.

Such connections suggest another important human duality, the personal and the communal. Language is a communal heritage to be used personally. Liturgy is a communal religious celebration to be entered into personally. The word of God in its liturgical character operates communally and personally for humanity. It was given to a people to become a people, a community of persons with personal gifts and responsibilities to be exercised in forming community.

Word and communications require an ethics that is personal and communal. Traditionally this has been an ethics of truth-telling, of not bearing false witness. The Hebrew origins of truth (*emeth*, fidelity of God to his word) and the New Testament concept of saving and liberating truth require a larger vision of word and truth for person and community. What we celebrate as the word and truth of God in liturgy must exercise its liberating kingdom function in the community of disciples, the church and in the larger human community. Personal authenticity, witnessing in word first of all to the truth that is in one, and witnessing before the others, telling the truth, is an inescapable demand of the gift of the truth.

Truth-telling as personal charge is not the whole of it. Truth-seeking and truth-sharing, as personal and communal, tasks belong just as much to the divine gift and human capacity. The ethics of truth for Christians insists on the seeking (e.g. freedom of research) and the sharing (e.g. freedom of information) in church and society in ways that often will be disturbing for power-holders. Stirring up the people with his kingdom-truth was one of the most serious charges against Jesus. His disciples may do no less. Liturgical celebrations of the word of God, by people who refuse these tasks of truth, deserve the age-old condemnations of Amos on 'such solemn assemblies' (Amos 5). To dare to proclaim the word of God in public is to take on a formidable task, which can be discharged only by somebody open to the grace of that word. 'Lord be merciful to me a sinner.'

Word and truth as community-building and person-developing take narrative form. Narrative, or origins and subsequent history, provides identity for community and person. The Hebrew and Christian scriptures perform that task for Christian community in its liturgy. Political and ethnic communities have their own narratives of origin and development. The Christian community narratives touch on human origins at their deepest and on human destiny at its furthest. They are faith-narratives shaping identity, and hope-narratives for a destiny which finally transcends (hi)story. Their truth does not conflict with the truth of other human narratives of origin (e.g. evolution, discovery and development of the Americas by Europeans) but it provides at once critique and transcendence. Purely human narratives of origin and destiny must be continually tested against the ultimate in the stories of God if they are not to become imprisoning ideologies like some forms of racism, nationalism and Marxism. The word in liturgy offers judgement as well as challenge and empowerment.

The truth of divine and human word is not only the truth of history. The stories on which communities are built may be larger than any modern concept of evidence warrants without declining into ideological packages. The creative storytellers of the past and present are liberatingly truthful in ways not measurable by the contemporary canons of history. The authors of the books of Genesis and of Job, of the Divine Comedy and Hamlet, have a range of liberating truth for the sensitive reader or listener. Creative word of God moves close to creative human word in its fictional, dramatic and poetic forms. Liturgy and literature have more in common than an indifferent reading of the word of God and an equally indifferent homily may often suggest. The historic relationship of drama and liturgy is only one part of an association that has enriched Christian liturgy and human culture over centuries. Christian life and liturgy must take seriously this connection of prayer and poetry in church and home, in school, theatre and concert hall, indeed wherever two or three gather together. This inter-connection concerns not just 'high culture' any more than it concerns just 'high' liturgy. Both liturgy and culture are essentially people's work. And the word of God did not come to any elite. It was the poor who were to have the gospel preached to them. The tension between the popular and the sophisticated in liturgy, as in literature, can be critical and creative for both.

The inauthentically high and the trivialising popular threaten language, living and liturgy in multiple ways. Christians as carriers of the word of God have their own responsibility to oppose the inauthentic and the trivial. A community whose communications are dominated by the trivial and the purely commercial (and inauthentic) is readily exposed to the living lie and beyond the reach of life-giving truth. When the trivial and the commercial combine to operate a pseudo-liturgy, Jesus is doubly denied before men. The word of God as a two-edged sword remains a permanent challenge to all genuine human communication in life and in liturgy.

V. Sacraments, society and environment

Word and sacrament are distinguishable but inseparable in celebration of Christian liturgy and in proclamation and promotion of God's kingdom. The distinction centres on the sacraments as symbolic actions by the community, as enacted and ritual remembering, realising and anticipating the work of God in Jesus Christ rather than simply verbal remembering. The words come too. Such enactment carries its own verbal narratives, songs of praise and words of blessing. As signs of the kingdom, sacraments are liturgical dramas in which the cast is the Christian community but the director and leading actor is Jesus Christ. Encountering Christ in the sacrament has been a form of theological short-hand since Edward Schillebeeckx' work in the 1950s, a period of considerable renewal in sacramental theology involving people like Schillebeeckx, Rahner and Semmelroth.

The transforming presence and power of God in cosmos and history, which Jesus proclaimed and inaugurated as God's kingdom, emerges in different forms in those actions of the Christian community called sacraments. The different forms relate to different stages and dimensions of Christian life and need. What is significant here is that they are directed to the in-breaking kingdom of God and so to the transformation of person and community in history and cosmos, a transformation to be completed, like the resurrection of Jesus, in transcending history.

Sacraments are then gifts and tasks of the kingdom. They are expressions of and resources for that transformation of humanity and cosmos which became available in the life, death and resurrection of Jesus Christ. They are personal and community activities with personal and community implications. In recent times they had become almost exclusively clerical in performance and individualist and passive in reception.

There was the clerical confessor and individual penitent in isolated confessional, or individual priest with isolated-in-public recipient of communion at the altar-rail. The essential community dimension of liturgy and sacraments had been obscured to the point of vanishing. The implications for life were equally serious. An individualist and sometimes trivialising morality prevailed: eating meat on Friday was on the same sinful level as adultery or murder. Person was diminished as well as community.

The thrust of the current liturgy of the sacraments is to promote personal participation and community celebration. The inherent tension of Christian and human living, personal differentiation in fuller community, is seen to cohere with the liturgical structures of encounter between God and humanity. The gifts and tasks of kingdom and humanity are revealed at their deepest in the sacraments. Person and community are judged in their failures, as well as healed and empowered for new life. For Christians, their ethical tasks in society and cosmos relate closely to their engagement with liturgical celebration of the sacraments.

Personal and community events, the sacraments have clear cosmos connection. Earthly elements, the matter of traditional theology, are integrated with the symbolic action and words into a unified mediating of the divine-human encounter. Water and oil, bread and wine, breath and fire, light and darkness, place and time, are recognised in their earthly reality and at the same time transformed into instruments of divine activity. Respect for the earth and its elements, required by the Christian stories of creation, acquires a deeper range and urgency with their sacramental role. Sacraments, as signs of the kingdom and so of God's design for the ultimate human community, also proclaim the current value and ultimate significance of planet earth and of the whole cosmos. A sacramental ecology is basic for Christians to an ecological ethics.

VI. Kingdom values and sacramental engagement

The fuller relationship of sacraments and Christian life in ethical terms may be best pursued by exploring the connections between individual sacraments and what are sometimes called kingdom values and virtues. These kingdom values and virtues derive from the biblical tradition of the kingdom in Hebrew and Christian scriptures. The primary kingdom values and virtues are faith-hope-love, taken as a dynamic, interconnecting triad in the Pauline fashion. They are both entrance values/virtues and continuance values/ virtues. To enter the kingdom and remain in it, faith-hope-love are essential. Christian life then is first of all a life of faith-hope-love. Christian liturgy and sacraments require and confer faith-hope-love. Christian community lives by faith-hope-love. Christian faith-hope-love must themselves be expressed and developed in Christian life, in what have been traditionally called the moral virtues. No entirely satisfactory classification or ordering of these is available. A crucial value and virtue for Christians, and one very akin to the primary virtue of faith, is that of truth and truthfulness already discussed. For biblical, sacramental and contemporary social reasons, three others are considered here: liberation and freedom; justice and equality; solidarity and peace. Their biblical and Christian background cannot be fully pursued here although it will emerge in discussing their connection with particular sacraments. Their contemporary social and political connections may be discerned by comparing them with the revolutionary political triad of the last two hundred years, *liberté, égalité, fraternité.*

(1) Liberation and Freedom

The coming of God's reign or kingdom constituted a liberating event for the Hebrews released from captivity in Egypt (Exodus), for Jesus' disciples offered the truth that would set them free (John), for the early Christians set free indeed (Gal 5, *et al*). This liberation from poverty, privation and prison (Lk 4, Is 61, *et al*), from sin, death and the law (Paul), has once again become a central concern in Christian life and theology. As effective signs of this liberation, of this kingdom both come and to come, the sacraments are to be celebrated by the Christian community as liberating events, liberating human beings to one another and to God. They form countersigns to oppression and enslavement, personal and communal. Baptism as the first sacrament of Christian life draws candidate(s) and community together in the liberating death and resurrection of Jesus, in the new exodus from slavery in Egypt. The liberating presence of God at baptism judges, challenges and empowers candidates and community to live together in freedom and to renounce the demons of oppression and exploitation. To celebrate baptism with Christ authentically, and to complete it in confirmation, community and candidate must be willing to go beyond the oppressions of race, class and sex. 'For as many of you as were baptised into Christ have put on Christ. There is neither Jew nor Greek, there is neither slave nor free, there is neither male nor female; for you are all one in Christ Jesus' (Gal 3:27f).

Other sacraments such as penance and eucharist offer their own witness to the liberating power of Jesus' death and resurrection. So does the sacrament of anointing in face of the spiritual, mental, emotional and physical ills to which humanity is heir. Embodiment and sexuality, interpreted too often in human history as entrapment for human beings, enjoy their own Christian liberation in the sacrament of marriage, symbol of the free surrender of Jesus Christ out of love for his friends (Eph 5). Freedom to serve the community liturgically and otherwise, and so the kingdom, is what is at issue in the sacrament of ordination. As that freedom cannot be restricted by race or class, one must question if it can be restricted by gender.

In sacramental theology today, the community-church is the primary sacrament, at once sacrament of Christ and of humanity transformed in Christ. It is as a liberated and liberating people that it is to be effective sign of the kingdom of God and of the new humanity. In liturgy the community-church acts precisely as such a sacrament of liberation. The individual sacraments must bear their own witness to this liberated and liberating community and so set the standard and provide the capacity for the divine and human work of liberation. The community-church is in turn challenged to be its sacramental self by the liberation movements abroad in the world.

(2) Justice and Equality

Justice (*sedaqah, dikaiosune*) is one of the central themes of the Hebrew and Christian scriptures, of the Mosaic covenant and the new covenant in Jesus Christ. The outcome of all that is described in another great Pauline word, 'justification,' making just parallel to liberation and setting free. The community of disciples, the primary sacrament, becomes the community of the just. What is to be witnessed and realised is the breakthrough of divine justice in human

person and community, the person and community which are Jesus
Christ.

Without rehearsing the relations to all the sacraments as with
liberation/freedom, it will be more useful to examine two aspects
of the biblical tradition of justice, equality and preference for the
poor. Created in the image of God, recreated in Jesus, the New
Adam, all human beings enjoy basic equality. Paul's rejection of
age-old division and discrimination in Galations 3:28 underlines
the impact of Jesus' dismissal of power and privilege to be replaced
by openness to the least. A certain paradox emerges here in Jesus'
levelling mission. Nobody is to lord it over other ('and yet the last
shall be first and the first last' – Mk 9:35). Jesus is picking up on the
divine strategy of Yahweh in his call of Israel, a fragmented group
of slaves lost in the imperial grandeur of Egypt. Indeed he is
rehearsing the strategy of Abba in choosing a marginal person and
place ('can anything good come out of Nazareth?' – Jn 1:46), and a
person destined to be rejected as a criminal on a cross, as the 'cor-
ner-stone' of the new temple, the kingdom come. To establish
equality in glory for all through identification with the poor and
deprived has been the strategy of Yahweh, Abba and Jesus. It must
remain the strategy of the community of disciples. The community's
liturgy and sacraments are intended as symbols of that strategy.

The interactions between liturgy/sacraments and equality/pref-
erential option for the poor in Christian life must be mutual. Each
dimension of liturgy and life is challenge and empowerment to the
other. The liberating effect of liturgy and sacraments discussed earlier relates closely to equality and preference for the poor. In more
political terms, human rights, which can be great protectors of the
weak, are human freedoms due in justice to persons. The overlap
between liberation, justice and preference for the poor has been critically developed in liberation theology. It may be less obvious in
Christian liturgy where wealth and power may be displayed and
indulged in counter-sacramental ways, at least where one is speaking of sacraments as effective signs of Christ. There is still much
need for dialogue on liturgy and Christian living before their implementation of Jesus' strategy is manifest and effective.

(3) Solidarity and Peace

For all its revolutionary resonance, *fraternité* has a certain hollow
ring today. This partly because, of the eighteenth-century triad, it is
one which has had least evident effect. The wars and massacres of

the twentieth century alone make a mockery of that eighteenth-century aspiration. The gender block also suggests a change in terminology. *Solidarity* has attained in current usage a sense close to *fraternité* and the biblical fellowship (*koinonia*). Responsibility for and to others, interdependence, living community, are all suggested by solidarity with its ecclesial and civil, national, international and even cosmic dimensions, all in the same ecological boat. Only one earth for the only one human community.

The biblical *shalom* suffered some impoverishment in the translation process: through *eirene, pax* and into *peace*. Originally it probably meant something like 'flourishing in communion' for Israel first and then for all the nations as well. It was both Yahweh's gift and Israel's (humanity's) task. It became in turn Jesus' gift ('My peace I leave with you' – Jn 14:27) and the disciples' task ('Blessed are the peace-makers' – Mk 5:9).

The relation between solidarity and peace in the sense of *shalom* is obvious and close. The gift which the community-church has received is also its kingdom task. The community of solidarity and *shalom* is to provide the pre-view, the first earnest (*arabon*, 2 Cor 1:22) of the final flourishing in communion. This *shalom* was promised to Israel and definitively offered in Jesus Christ. This community is called and empowered to be sacrament of solidarity and *shalom*. In its self-manifestation and self-realisation in the liturgy and in the individual sacraments, its peace-giving and peace making character, is to be manifest and realised. It is to be sacramentalised.

Eucharist and penance have clear peace-giving and peace-making capacities. They are both, in the traditional sense, sacraments of reconciliation, even if their forms of celebration have not always made that clear. In the interchange between liturgy and Christian life this reconciliation dimension has been frequently over-individualised: 'my sin, my confession, my God, my forgiveness.' Social division, oppression and sinfulness have been obscured. More seriously, the administration of the sacraments and the call for reconciliation have too often endorsed deeply divisive and oppressive conditions. Performing signs of reconciliation, without any conversion of heart and structure, renders these sacramental signs futile. God is mocked and humanity is more deeply injured. Christian life in genuine search of peace and solidarity will challenge, with Amos, such inauthentic liturgy.

VII. Communion in a consuming universe

Christian life and liturgy occur in the context of sin and evil. The great symbols of God's achievement in Israel and Jesus, liberation, salvation, redemption, justification, new creation, make clear this presence of evil to be overcome. Jesus' own suffering and death which are basic to Christian life and liturgy, ('if anyone will come after me' – Mk 8:34; 'Do this in remembrance of me' – Lk 22:19), confirm the reality of evil in the world and the need to overcome it. The book of Job wrestles with one of the most poignant and puzzling aspects of evil in the world: why do the innocent suffer? The power of that book rests eventually in its acceptance of the mystery of this suffering but set off against the transcendent power and goodness of God. The passion and resurrection narratives in the New Testament follow much the same pattern. Suffering is real and puzzling, in Jesus' case (and in many other cases) undeserved. But out of that goodness may come, as the loving and creative power of God prevails. And the final enemy, death, has been overcome in God's raising Jesus to life as first fruits for all.

Liturgy properly insists on the goodness of God and creation in psalm and hymn, prayer and creating, saving narrative. Praise and thanksgiving are primary liturgical functions. So are they primary functions of Christian life. Yet the tragic dimension of life continues to assert itself and to demand liturgical response. In the liturgies of forgiveness and of entrusting the dead to their merciful God, this tragic dimension finds some response. Yet the pervasiveness and depth of evil in the world, its connection with the very dynamism of life itself, has not been fully addressed so far in this examination of liturgy and life.

'God looked on the world and saw that it was good.' After the creation of humankind, 'that it was very good.' Yet this becomes rapidly the world of evil and sin, of human division ('she did it'), alienation from nature, fratricide (Cain and Abel), breakdown of all communications (Babel) (Genesis 1-11). The fertile myths of Genesis and other Hebrew works were struggling to reconcile the good work of a good creator with the undoubted presence of destruction and evil. Job undertook the most searching examination of this puzzle in life and thought and, while he banished the easy answers, he too had to bow before the mystery.

In a different world with it own fertile, truth-bearing myths, such as evolution, and its own potent, destructive myth of consumerism, a rather different symbolic and imaginative effort may be needed to relate evil to Christian life and liturgy. Something analogous was attempted by Pierre Teilhard de Chardin (*The Hymn of the Universe*). His emphasis was on the predominantly good creative and evolving world, with less attention to the inter-weaving evil. One of his great liturgical images was his 'Mass on the world,' a eucharist of the universe, a fitting anticipatory sign for his vision of the coming kingdom in the emerging Christogenesis. The richness of his vision remains to be developed in various ways by the Christian community in its life and liturgy.

A less simply hopeful, less optimistic vision than that of Teilhard de Chardin would undoubtedly look with awe and respond with praise to the created masterpiece of our physical and human world. It would also look more closely and less uncritically at the consuming, destroying, nature of the world.

In what Teilhard called the biosphere, the sphere of living things or the chain of life as it is called in ecological terms, the dynamism of survival and growth is that of consumption. All living beings live off other living beings. To survive is to consume the others. Such consumption extends, as certain environment crises indicate, from that of the ozone layer to that of fossil, from the living to non-living. We live in a self-consuming universe. And it is no decisive mark of human difference that we as humans may consume non-human or sub-human reality and avoid consumption ourselves. In the end we too are consumed. From dust to dust. Earth-consumers, we are finally consumed by earth. And in the interim we humans are frequently busy consuming one another. The necessary and natural consuming of the baby at its mother's breast has its own beauty and value. The malice or weakness which issues in adults or even children consuming one another, from the most intimate relations of marriage and family to more distant but no less potent relationships of politics and commerce, provides so many modern parables of sin. Natural consumption, with its inevitable killings and dying for plants, animals and humans, reaches the new human sphere of tragedy and sin in human hatred and war, power-seeking and oppression, self-indulgence and other-destruction. What we may lightly call a consumerist world is deeply pervasive of us all in continuity with structures of the universe. The culling of seals has its parallels in the periodic culling of humans we call war or massacre. The dignity, freedom, equality and solidarity, for which humans are created in the Jewish and Christian vision, reveal their own tragic role in self-destruction.

The history of Yahweh's relation with Israel marks a struggle to overcome human self-destructiveness within what remained a consuming universe. Israel's consumption of the prophets, God's messengers, drew Yahweh further into the self-giving task of forming this people as God's own people, from there to all people as God's. Last of all God sent God's son (Heb 1). The entry of God in Jesus into this destructive and consuming universe was the final challenge. As human, Jesus was a consumer from his mother's breast, through childhood and adolescent needs to table-fellowship with publicans and sinners.

His person and ministry were directed beyond the inevitable and necessary biological consumption: with 'living water' by which one will never thirst, for the Samaritan woman (Jn 4); for the disciples 'fruit for eternal life' (Jn 4) and 'the bread which comes down from heaven' (Jn 6). In the more mundane synoptic accounts, he confronts consuming and consumed humanity by feeding the hungry, healing the sick, raising the widow's son, forgiving sinners. All these are signs of the kingdom, of the new presence and power of God which could overcome the trap of simply consuming and being consumed. Not yet though. Not until he himself was drawn into the circle of malicious human consumption, betrayed and deserted by his closest friends, mocked and tortured, given a show trial, had a notorious criminal preferred to him, unjustly sentenced and cruelly executed. The savage consumerism of the powers and the powerless, the political and religious leaders and the mob, could indulge their consuming lust in his passion and death.

God had died, had been consumed by human destructiveness. *Consummatum est.* It was all over. Yet the night before he died 'as they were eating, Jesus took bread, and blessed, and broke it, and gave it to the disciples and said: "Take, eat: this is my body." And he took a cup, and when he had given thanks he gave it to them saying, "Drink of it; for this is my blood of the covenant, which is poured out for many for the forgiveness of sins"' (Mt 26) .

'And after the sabbath, toward the dawn of the first day of the week, Mary Magdalene and the other Mary went to see the sepulchre ... the angel said to the women: "Do not be afraid: for I know that you seek Jesus who was crucified. He is not here; for he has risen, as he said"' (Mt 28).

Jesus' passion narrative is framed by the last supper and the resurrection. His gift of himself to his disciples in bread and wine, his body and blood, in memory of him, until he comes again, is the critical acceptance and transcendence of our human consumption of one another. Consumption must yield to communion at least in symbol. The ultimate reality of that symbol, of communion beyond all consumption, only emerges with the resurrection of Jesus. When consumption had done its worst in death, indeed in killing unto death, the life-giving power of God raised Jesus to communion with God and with all in ways which human destructiveness could never again touch. The age of natural and sinful consumption had been conquered in the dying and rising of Jesus. The symbol, the sacrament of that conquest had already been given in eucharist. The central liturgical act of the community of disciples became a gift of communion to enable communion to overcome consumption. The final overcoming must wait until he comes again. Doing this in memory of him establishes communion now in and through the very consumption of the elements, of the body and blood of Christ. By taking consumption on at its most destructive, Jesus has shown how symbolically or sacramentally, in a life nourished by liturgy, communion may be sustained in a world still dependent on controlled consumption, but exposed to the temptations of uncontrolled, self-indulgent and exploitative consumption.

VIII. In the End God: The *Danse Macabre* and *Perichoresis*

Liturgy and Christian life belong to history but are not confined by it. The irruption of God into human history has opened it up to the transhuman, the transcendent and the eschatological. The coming of the kingdom now eschatologically shapes Christian life and liturgy in many significant ways. Both are expressions of hope for final liberation to one another and to God, for ultimate flourishing in communion, a communion that completely transcends consumption. Liturgy and life look to resurrection and to eternal life, life with God and with one another in eternal fulfilment. In the end, God. Of course, in the beginning God also. And in the interim, God who became human, who took on the conditions of history and surrendered to the consuming universe to establish true communion.

God thus proved to be a communion God for creation but also for the creator. The community of God which was gradually revealed/discerned was the mystery of triune God. Yahweh, the God of Israel and of Christians, emerged for Christians as triune, one God in three persons: Abba/Father; Word/Son/Redeemer; Spirit/Sanctifier.

In liturgy and in life it is possible to worship the one God, saying 'Abba' in Christ, by the Spirit's gift of daughterhood and sonship. In concept and language, the triune God is less easy to deal with. Further connecting points with the mystery may be developed in liturgical celebration and Christian living by attesting to the character of communion within God and its exemplary and empowering force for those created in God's image.

The traditional doctrine of the Trinity as it developed in the early centuries stressed the differentiation, the equality and the unity. Many theologians see in this a model for human community with differentiation, equality and unity, keeping close to freedom, equality and fraternity, in both their recent political and more ancient biblical senses. A trinitarian shaped liturgy addressed to Abba through Christ by the Spirit provides in turn a model and power for human society. Developments in freedom, equality and solidarity in human society make the divine image in humanity more evident and challenge liturgy to do likewise.

In the idiom of consumption and communion, the triune God forms dynamic communion without consumption. This is the eschatological operating in history. What Jesus did, what we recall in liturgy, what we attempt in living, is to realise the communion that breaks through the destructive circle of consumption that the divine communion may be shared with all, that God may be 'all in all.'

The Eastern tradition had a term for the dynamic triunity of God, which may take us a little further. *Perichoresis* referred to God's dynamic community in terms of the dance, the moving, harmonious and loving interchange of the three persons. Dance sometimes figures significantly in liturgy. As image for liturgy and life, it is rich in possibilities. Connecting the divine *perichoresis* with the dance or the loving musical movements of liturgy and with the harmonious, loving movements of life at its best, can illuminate the gifts and tasks of Christians. The invitation to the dance *perichoresis*, is offered in history. But the offer is never closed. The historical dance may not be self-enclosing. The range of partners is all humankind. The poor, the sick, the racially or sexually excluded, all these must be sought out by Christians to be genuine partners in the dance of life. Only thus will the *danse macabre* be replaced by *perichoresis*. Liturgy and Christian life are enabled and called to be exhibitions and expressions of that dance of life. Together, in mutual confirmation, challenge and empowerment, they create a widening circle of human involvement in the dance of God.

CHAPTER 11

Theology in a time of AIDS

Theology is always in time, its narrative character underlines that. The human enterprise of theology can be developed only over time. Out of time, before and beyond there is no need for theology and no possibility of narrative. All that, apparently reasonable discourse hinges on the nature of time, which remains finally as mysterious to us as it was to Augustine. The two key Greek words for time, *chronos* and *kairos*, continue to be helpful in distinguishing time as objective and measurable, what is now called clock time, and time which is subjectively significant for person or community. *Kairos* is in that sense storied time. In Jewish and Christian terms *kairos* indicates a time and event of divine call for human response. So it was with the prophets and Jesus' announcement of the reign of God. This was the *Kairos*, the time of God's special presence and summons.

These two, *chronos* and *kairos*, may be distinguished but not separated. The time-laden character of theology involves both. Change in theology as in everything human is related to the ticking clock at least in its biological form. The significance of that change relates to human subjects and their capacity to read the signs of the time. To speak of theology in a time of AIDS is to consider the (chronological) time-span from the first (recent) diagnosis of AIDS in 1981 into the 1990s and its subsequent development into a global pandemic but it is to do more than that. How much more only the finished article will tell.

'Theology in a Time of AIDS' has some of the melodramatic ring of the title of Marquez' novel *Love in the Time of Cholera*. There is certainly drama but tragedy rather than melodrama in the AIDS story of the last ten or twelve years. However, why pick out AIDS as theologically significant? Why not cholera or tuberculosis, rampant again in a new resistant form? And why give theological significance to any time characterised by major diseases or other crisis? Did we have theology for the time of the Black Death or any of the

great wars? Not in so many words perhaps. But the prophets of
Israel, Jesus himself and great religious thinkers and theologians
from Augustine to Barth have sought to respond to the crises of
their times as particular calls from God. It is perhaps only a recent
fashion to name the crisis and bracket theology with it, as a
'Theology for a Nuclear Age'. The tradition of addressing fresh
human crises theologically or in a reflective religious way is much
longer and stronger.

The extent and depth of the pandemic suggests a major world
crisis. UNAIDS figures suggest that by June 1996 the cumulative
figure for cases of AIDS in adults and children, which were officially
reported to the WHO, was 1,393,649, representing an increase of
approxiamtely 19% over the figure for June 1995. However, because
of under-recognition and under-reporting, it is estimated that more
than 7.7 million cases have actually occurred since the epidemic
started. UNAID estimates that more than 3.1 million new HIV
infections will occur during 1996, or more than 8,500 a day. During
1995, HIV/AIDS-associated illnesses caused the deaths of 1.3 million people, including 300,000 children under five years of age.
Overall, there were 21.8 million people living with HIV/AIDS in
June 1996, and approximately 42% of them were women, a proportion which was increasing. The majority of newly-infected adults
were between 15 and 24 years old.

Of equal importance to the figures are the rate and range of
growth. The former beliefs that this was a disease of gay men and
IV drug-users (through their own fault for some commentators)
have had to yield to the recognition that heterosexual intercourse is
now the more common means of transmission and that no group of
whatever class or race, gender or sexual orientation is immune to
infection by HIV.

These numbers have meanings that no mere digits could convey. The meanings emerge in the stories of individuals, families
and whole societies devastated by the fears, the sufferings and the
deaths experienced throughout the world over the last decade and
more. To appreciate the real challenge to theology in a time of AIDS
it is necessary to listen to these stories and their tellers, persons with
AIDS themselves, the HIV infected their families, partners, lovers,
carers. More illuminating still for theologians would be engagement with the struggle in the praxis of caring for and suffering with
with. On the basis of such stories and praxis, of co-suffering or compassion, fresh analysis may be possible and new understanding
emerge.

Some of these stories formed the basis of theological reflection for a Commission organised by Caritas Internationalis (CI), the world-wide confederation of national Catholic social service and development organisations which has been co-operating with local initiatives around the world in seeking to harness Catholic and Christian responses to the challenges of HIV and AIDS. In contexts as diverse as North America and South-East Asia, the Caribbean, Europe and Africa this group has been at once learning and teaching by listening to, critiquing and retelling the stories, the analyses and the practices it has itself encountered. The reflections outlined here an attempt to mediate between these encounters and the Catholic theological tradition. Unfortunately the richly storied background to the reflections cannot be presented in detail here.

A world crisis and its harrowing and heroic stories of human suffering require Christian response and reflection, some fresh theological consideration. The HIV/AIDs crisis has some distinctive characteristics beyond its global range and savage suddenness, as ti brings together in such devastating mix the great human powers of sex and death. How this mix affects theology and in particular moral theology will be a primary concern of this chapter.

Retelling, reflecting and rereading

The short if substantial story of the AIDS/HIV pandemic and the comparatively slight story of the CI group's activity provoke in the telling and retelling reflection on the Christian traditions which sustain and inspire the group. The retelling and the reflection issue in rereading of the Christian scriptures and traditions which may reveal omissions or misunderstandings or at least open the way to fresh and fuller understanding. Liberation theologies of the Latin American, black and feminist kinds are only the most recent examples of how serious social challenges with their new questions on human meanings and morals have compelled serious and fruitful rereading of these scriptures and traditions. It would be rash to claim at this stage at any rate that AIDS/HIV could have far-reaching implications for the practice of theology and the understanding of Christian faith. The experience of liberation theologies should, however, alert us to understanding the impact of the pandemic on Christian thinking and practice and above all preclude reducing the discussion to marginal if genuinely important details like the use of condoms or exchange of needles in programmes of prevention. The questions for theology raised by AIDS/HIV may not be confined within the conventional limits of moral theology. Their questions for moral theology go well beyond the tabloid writers' concerns with condoms and needles. (The Tabloid mentality is not always restricted to journalists.) The theological rereading undertaken here examines central issues of Christian belief and living before it takes up some of the significant details in their proper Christian context.

Divine presence and power

Theology is first of all about God. Discussion of theology in a time of AIDS must begin with God. It is plausible to hold that the pandemic raises no new questions about God and indeed, as Leslie Houlden argues, no new theological questions at all. At least it raises some old questions in new and for the persons immediately involved in very acute forms. The Book of Job may constitute the most profound reflection we have on the relation between human suffering and divine presence in power. Indeed Job's own bodily sufferings and attendant mental anguish and anger may awaken painful echoes in contemporary readers wrestling with the impact of AIDS/HIV. Yet new generations of sufferers with a different ethos of religious belief/doubt and personal, cultural or even medical expectations will experience ultimate questions in quite different ways.

Job's confrontation with the mysterious God of the whirlwind, with his claim to creative laying of the foundations of the earth and to the powerful differentiation of animal life, leaves him awe and humbled before the presence and power of his creator and vindicator/redeemer. He has won his argument with his confrere comforters. Personal sin is not the cause of his suffering and he is not being punished by God for such sin. The lesson must be continually repeated and the Book of Job read again and again in face of those Christians who still think of human suffering in terms of God's punishment for personal sin and see a particularly apt application of this doctrine in the emergence of AIDS/HIV.

The presence and power of God in the whirlwind do not resolve all the difficulties. They do, however, open us up to the finally mysterious ways of God in creation and providence. These ways take a radically new turn in Jesus Christ. The power and the presence, whose time (*kairos*) has come in Jesus' proclamation of the kingdom or reign of God, offer a very different response to human suffering from the whirlwind proclamation. Leaving aside Jesus' own ministry to the sick, to which we will return, we are confronted with the mystery of God entering fully into the human condition, even to the point of taking on human suffering and dying in the passion and death of Jesus Christ. The crucial and cruciform revelation of God's co-suffering (compassion) with human beings in Jesus manifests a new aspect of the mystery we also call love. It is not simply comprehensible to us, but it does reassure us about the presence. 'Where are you God as I am overcome by the pain and desperation?' 'Right here with you just as I was on Calvary.' And the power, the omnipotence as we used to say? No more absent or frustrated than on Calvary but taking its mysterious ways through creaturely and bodily fragility to a healing in love and life that may or may not issue in renewed bodily life and health. The inexhaustible loving which endured through Calvary does not abandon those for whom Calvary was undertaken in the first place.

Jesus and the Kingdom

Jesus and his God are not to be understood simply in terms of the passion and death on Calvary. These undoubtedly form the climax to his life and mission as they do the gospel narratives. Yet they are only properly and fully understood in the light of Jesus' public life and ministry, by which he pursued his mission and encountered his destiny. By the announcement of the kingdom or reign of God which opened the ministry and specified the mission Jesus at once confirmed and transformed the tradition of Israel. The kingdom motif in Israel anticipated a restoration of a Davidic style kingdom with the God of Israel, Yahweh, newly present in all his power and glory. The presence in power which Jesus offered in the name of his Father was no less glorious for those with eyes to see but it paradoxical character defeated the perception of many contemporaries.

This was not a kingdom first of all for the powerful and wealthy, who were to be toppled from their seats and sent empty away. The sinners and the prostitutes, the poor and the socially marginalised like the lepers and the tax gatherers would go first into the kingdom. By indetifying with these, by eating and drinking with them Jesus overturned the accepted canons of religious and political respectability. It was eventually to cost him his life as he was considered too subversive of the established order and after a show trial was crucified between two other criminals outside the gates of the city. Exclusion had reached its terminus in criminalisation and execution for him who would make the excluded the centre of his mission. For Christians who feel the urge to reject or avoid or neglect people living with AIDS/HIV the counter-example of Jesus should be a forceful reminder. As we do it to one of these least ones.

Jesus did not simply seek the company of the excluded, he did see that as a way of establishing a new set of relationships, a new kind of community, a new Israel which would embody the kingdom of God which he announced. In this new community God's presence and power would be evident above all in the practices of love. And it would be effective love, feeding the hungry, setting the prisoners free, restoring sight to the blind, letting the lame walk, healing all manner of sickness. Jesus' ministry to the sick has inspired generations of Christians. He explicitly rejected the old mistake of Job's comforters. 'Neither this man nor his parents have sinned,' he told his disciples of the man born blind. In this case as in others the healing manifested the power and the glory of God by attending to immediate needs of the suffering and excluded. The new Israel would also be a new creation with the God-given powers of creation restored and fulfiled. In Christian care and human scientific development these God-given resources are to be harnessed in restoration of health and comfort of the afflicted. Love after the manner of Jesus unconditional acceptance and care of the needy, must be expressed in the most effective way possible, medically, socially and personally.

Moral Theology and Natural Law

The community of disciples which follows Jesus and seeks to proclaim and promote his kingdom of God in the world for the healing/transformation of the world, must act in imitation of Jesus, sharing his heart and mind. The reading and rereading of that mind and its thoughtful application to the needy and excluded of a particular time form that part of the permanent theological task called moral theology or Christian ethics. It is a task that must be approached thoughtfully using the resources of God-given minds after the fashion of Augustine, Aquinas, Barth and all the other great Christian thinkers. It can never treat the mind in separation from heart and action but it must be true to its gifts and limitations. Over the millennia Christian, Jewish and indeed pagan minds have contributed powerfully to elucidating how Christians might act individually and socially in imitation of Christ. The more systematic attempts to do this have issued in different if related theologies which were distinguished at a later period in the Catholic tradition (c. 1600) as moral theology. It has never been an entirely satisfactory distinction, particularly when it hardened into sharp division. It was a distinction unknown to Augustine and Aquinas. Here the focus will be on some systematic outline of Christian living according to the mind of Christ without losing touch with the biblical narratives or later doctrinal insights and developments.

Catholic moral theology has been dominated over the centuries by the concept of natural law. With a certain biblical basis and a strong base in the western philosophical tradition it has proved of enormous value both in the development of systematic thinking about Christian morals and in dealing with particular cases. In CI's ventures into areas of very limited Christian background in Asia and Africa this same natural law approach offered a first step, if only a first, in seeking some mutual moral understanding on AIDS/HIV with people of quite different religious and cultural backgrounds. For Catholics and people sharing a similar philosophical background it will continue to sustain and illuminate moral analysis. The absence of what Alasdair MacIntyre might term any public moral consensus can make the claims made for natural law from a Church or theological background seem arbitrary or simply the diktats of authority without any real basis in the reason to which it pretends. The current criticisms of the Enlightenment enthronement of reason make natural law arguments harder to sustain outside a limited Catholic circle. The approach adopted here is not therefore directly based on natural law arguments. The sources are more immediately biblical and theological. Yet it will undoubtedly overlap with and be nourished by the content of the natural law tradition in its structural design and case-discussion.

Kingdom values and moral virtues

The new presence and power of God realised in the life and ministry, death and resurrection of Jesus Christ is another description of the kingdom of God which he declared fulfiled in his time (*kairos*), fulfiled that is in relation to the promises his people of Israel had received and the expectations they had developed. A paradoxical and disconcerting kingdom may be drawn from Jesus' teaching and ministry as well as from his death and resurrection and his immediate disciples' response. However, even a cursory reading of Jesus' parables of the kingdom reveals how obscure or rather mysterious it remains. Inevitably so when one is speaking of the presence and power of God, creating and sustaining, enabling and healing, fulfiling and transforming humanity and the cosmos; to essay a further but still beggarly description of the mystery which we inhabit and which inhabits us.

The kingdom of God is about us and within us, in Jesus' own words, seeks and enables our recognition, our expression and manifestation of it, our participation in its development. As we are called in the Genesis narrative to participate in God's original creative activity, so we are called in the Jesus narrative to participate in God's new creative activity. But who are the 'we' who are called? The 'we' must match the range of creation and new creation. The 'we' is first and last of all humankind. It is only the community of Jesus' disciples who can explicitly recognise the kingdom. But the kingdom is for all human beings and above all by Jesus' example and teaching for the least of our human sisters and brothers, meaning the least by the standards of the worldly world, the poor, the socially excluded, the sick, who in a time and place of AIDS can so easily coincide. So the disciples of Jesus, as entrusted with the vision and enabling call of the kingdom, must offer a lead in responding to these least ones by active caring, loving personal relationships and structural reform.

The anticipation of Jesus' vision of God's kingdom which the Hebrew prophets in particular proclaimed provides a basis for a moral structuring of the kingdom call as it affects the Christian lives of disciples and the moral goals of the whole human community. While this is primarily a biblical and theological approach it will have evident connections with a natural law approach. It is not the only biblical/theological approach possible but it may be quite illuminating in relating morally the kingdom of God to human society in this time of AIDS/HIV.

As I have already developed the discussion of kingdom values more fully elsewhere I will deal rather briefly with them here. Within the biblical-theological tradition it is possible to discern a range of values which are to be realised in the presence and through the power of God. Some of these express the presence and power of Godself in stories of Israel and of Jesus. Characteristic of God in covenant they are to characterise human beings in covenant with one another as well as with God. They embody the very presence and power of God in personal interaction and social structure. In that created and creative dialect of person and society kingdom values foreshadow fulfilment of person and society, the thrust of God's successive covenants. The realisation of these values, however partial, is a realisation of the kingdom in its historical limitations. In another philosophical idiom they may provide a basis for a vision of society which connects with traditions other than the Jewish and Christian.

The four kingdom values which seem to serve these theological and philosophical purposes are those of truth, freedom, justice and peace (*shalom*). They may also be called primary kingdom values because they reflect the primary reality of God. Other values which do not reflect God immediately may be termed secondary. This does not make them unimportant but simply states that they are not in themselves characteristic of God. Values related to our embodied condition such as chastity are not directly applicable to God and so are secondary in this sense.

Presence and power of God in truth

The pursuit of Pilate's question 'what is truth?' in its current hermeneutical complexities is a task for another time and place. Truth is central to the Jewish and Christian traditions, as central as God. It is God. More accurately and profoundly God is truth. The ultimate reality revealing itself is basic truth for humanity, at once summoning and enabling human beings to recognise the truth and to live by it. Only by listening to the God-given call to truth, by seeking and at least partially attaining the truth and striving to do it or live by it can human being live with one another. The dialectic of person and society demands minimal truthfulness for its minimal successful resolution. Such minimal achievement is an expression of the kingdom, of the presence and power of God.

Social and personal crises like war and the pandemic AIDS/HIV threaten truth. At least without continuous commitment to truth the crisis will be misunderstood and the response mistaken. The temptation to conceal the truth of the extent of the pandemic is one aspect of how the threat may aggravate the crisis. Fears of contagion by family, friends and carers based on untruth can readily undermine social and personal responses. Only the truth in the gospel phrase will set us free to deal effectively with the crisis. And it is the divinely begotten hunger for truth which may hope through research to find medical means of prevention and cure.

Quite complex problems of confidentiality and information can arise for people living with AIDS/HIV, for their partners and carers, medical and social. How the truth is respected and in the context of personal rights to privacy and dignity and of social need may not be easily discerned. The other kingdom values of freedom, justice and peace/solidarity will play a role here as they will in handling most moral dilemmas arising from the pandemic. Beyond that it is important to recognise that kingdom values do not come cheaply.

Truth like grace will often be costly. It is the responsibility of the community of disciples, of witnesses to the kingdom, to ensure with Jesus Christ that the cost is shared and the heavier burden of it borne by those in the best position to pay.

Presence and power of God in freedom

The freedom of God in creation and covenant forms the basis of human freedom of choice as well as of the progressive liberation of person and society which the kingdom of God seeks, enables and achieves if only partially in history. In the messianic programme announced by Jesus in Luke 4 the basis of kingdom liberation is already set. With prisoners to go free, the blind to see, the lame to walk and the poor to receive the good news of the kingdom, the basic enslavements of the human condition, personal and social, sacred and profane in sin and oppression are to be overcome. The freedom of the children of God is at once gift and task. The maturing of person and society so that each person and each society is gradually enabled to harness itself and its resources in creative self-expression and other-service indicates the human shape of kingdom liberation.

In face of the pandemic the search for freedom from further infection through effective and humane preventive measures is an essential response to the kingdom call. Development of therapeutic measures connects the kingdom call to truth and its call to free people from the slavery of disease. And freedoms may well clash here or certainly appear to clash. Programmes of mandatory testing for so called risk groups or of quarantine for people with AIDS/HIV are usually unfair restriction of people already restricted socially or physically. Here the cross-over between freedom and justice emerges in human rights or liberties. In quite a different manner freedom and maturity emerge for the sexually active as forming the basis for the integration of sexuality into personal maturity in relating to other sexual beings. The interrelation of the primary kingdom values with one another and their influence in shaping the secondary values must be continually kept in mind.

Presence and power of God in justice

For many biblical scholars justice is the central description of God in the scriptures, particularly in the Hebrew scriptures. A more popular but inaccurate analysis would contrast the God of justice in the Hebrew scriptures and covenant with the God of love in the

Christian scriptures and new covenant. In both scriptures the justice of God is the shape which the love of God, or better, the love that is God, takes in covenantal saving relationship with the errant Israel and sinful humanity.

Divine justice characterises God's commitment to and responsibility for the world and for humanity through the covenants of creation, with Abraham and Moses, and in Jesus Christ. That commitment and responsibility require and enable human commitment and responsibility to and for one another. The great prophets of justice in eighth-century Israel (BCE) denounced as unacceptable to God assemblies of worshippers who neglected the widow, the orphan and the stranger, the judges who refused justice to the poor (cf. Amos). For Jeremiah faith in God is primarily expressed in justice. In more contemporary language recognition of, respect for and response to the human others is the test of authentic recognition of the ultimate other. The fairness and equality which justice demands focuses in both old and new testament versions of God's kingdom on the deprived and excluded. The blessed who hunger and thirst after justice as disciples of Jesus will be judged, rendered justice themselves on how far they fed and cared for these least ones. To feed and care for them is to care for Jesus, the incarnate ultimate other.

In a more analytic mode justice is distinguished as personal and social, as regulating fairness in relations between individual persons and in structural relations within society. Many of the problems revealed by the pandemic are problems of justice, personal and social. Some of these may be adequately expressed in terms of human rights and pursued in that fashion. However, not all delicate justice problems may be translated into human rights language without considerable loss of moral impact. Issues of testing, for example, may be usefully treated in terms of rights but there are cases such as mandatory testing of candidates for admission to seminaries and religious orders where larger concerns like witness may also need consideration. Here the interconnection between kingdom values emerges as freedom and justice overlap in rights, and truth and peace overlap in witness.

Presence and power of God in peace

Peace is a much neglected theme in theology and particularly in moral theology, where it barely figured as a side-issue in the just war discussion. Yet it is a central to the survival of the human race.

The presence and power of God to be realised and manifest in genuine peace between and within individuals, between and within societies, constitutes the most profound kingdom challenge facing the disciples of Jesus Christ today. In the biblical tradition peace, shalom in Hebrew, far exceeds the minimalist absence of war or maintenance of law and order, the pax romana. Flourishing in communion might be much better description of the peace anticipated in the kingdom and offered by Jesus to his disciples and through them to the world. It incorporates both ideas of flourishing in unity or solidarity with implications of truth, freedom and justice. It also involves the more specifically Christian themes of healing, reconciliation and forgiveness.

The AIDS/HIV pandemic should stimulate then a much needed development in understanding and promoting the kingdom value of peace. The dimensions of solidarity, healing, reconciling and forgiving have obvious relevance for both the personal and social challenges of AIDS/HIV. Their understanding and application here will provide insight into other peace needs and possibilities.

Kingdom values and sexuality

The presence and power of God which Jesus announced as the kingdom involves personal, social and cosmic transformation. In seeking to express in moral terms the significance of the kingdom four structural values were selected as primary for their biblical roots, their structural role in moral living and above all their attribution to Godself in Hebrew and Christian tradition. Other moral values which by these criteria are described as secondary have their own biblical roots, their role in moral living and a relationship, however indirect, to God. Yet the primary values will shape these secondary values in ways to be explored. Of immediate concern here is the value associated with sexuality, the value of chastity and how it is influenced by the primary values.

That God was not sexually described or defined was a notable and distinctive achievement of Hebrew religion. However, the origins and development of human sexuality were related by that tradition in its own distinctive way to God's creative presence and power. In one Genesis account (Gen 1) when God created humanity, 'male and female he created (it), in the image of God he created them'. For love and companionship, for life-giving and co-creating this gift of sexual duality was given to humans as images of God. This kind of human loving, sexual loving is celebrated in itself as gift in the Song of Songs. In other biblical writings it is recognised as mirroring God's love for Israel (Hosea, Isaiah) and as a sacrament or sign of Christ's love for the Church, the community of his disciples. A Christian theological view of sexuality has no place for the 'sex is dirty' syndrome.

The divine gift of sexuality implies a human call and task. The goals of loving and life-giving, broader human goals are specified more exactly in sexuality. These goals have to be sought over time by the development and integration of a person's sexual endowment into a fuller personal, relational and social life. The Catholic and Christian tradition with its biblical foundation sees the climax of that development emerging in marriage. Full sexual expression of the whole person belongs in this tradition to the established and yet developing community of love of one man and one woman which is open to new life. The kingdom value of truth with its associates of fidelity and honesty belongs to and protects this sacramental community as the Catholic tradition describes it. Freedom is essential to the origins of such a commitment as the freedom interrogation at the beginning of the marriage rite confirms. Justice belongs in different ways to the fulfilment of the marriage call. The injustice element in adultery provides one example of this. Without peace and its unitive, reconciling and forgiving dimensions marriage would not exist or survive.

The Christian community and the Catholic Church also recognise the sexual endowment and kingdom call of the unmarried, the single, the celibate and the widowed. Indeed celibacy for the sake of the kingdom has played a significant, sometimes a dominating, role in relating kingdom and sexuality. The 'perfect' chastity of the celibate calling was contrasted with the 'imperfect' of marriage. Celibates and other unmarried people are not asexual and not automatically and statically chaste. Chastity is not something a person is born with and with a bit of luck hangs on to. No moral value or associated virtue is like that. People become chaste, as indicated above, by gradually integrating their sexual gifts into responses appropriate to the different relationships in their lives, husband-wife, parent-child, brother-sister, friends, neighbours, colleagues, acquaintances. So celibates and other unmarried people are called to grow into the value and virtue of chastity. In this growth the primary kingdom values will protect and promote the value of chastity for the unmarried as they do for married people. It must be admitted, however, that little specific positive elaboration for growth into chastity by the unmarried exists in the Christian moral tradition. Moral theologians and teachers have usually settled for the simple negative guidelines – no intercourse outside marriage. Reducing the whole sexual life to intercourse is not particularly helpful to married people either. Celibates and singles, heterosexual and homosexual, need more help than that if they are to become dynamically chaste. They too are called to be people whose sexuality promotes loving and life-giving/enriching relationships as signs and realisations of the presence and power of God. Some further consideration will be given to this in the later sections.

Christian ministry and morality

With the biblical-theological background sketched here and in the context of the ministry promoted by Caritas Internationalis in response to the pandemic, it may help to focus the discussion of practical moral issues in terms of Christian ministry. In this way particular issues are related to the personal ministry of Jesus in the gospels, and to the ministry of the community of disciples in discerning and promoting the kingdom, with their emphasis on the deprived and excluded. The moral distortions which Jesus criticised for imposing insupportable burdens on the weak may be more readily apparent and avoided.

In structuring these brief notes on some of the moral issues raised by AIDS/HIV in the context of Christian ministry, only four aspects of ministry are considered, companionship, care, analysis of typical cases or casuistry and education. As aspects of ministry to the kingdom they assume acceptance of kingdom values, primary and secondary.

Companionship

Jesus' recognition and inclusion, to the point of table-fellowship, of the poor and excluded provides the model for Christian ministry to people with AIDS/HIV. The first moral response of disciples must be to accompany the ill and infected. Without unconditional acceptance and persistent accompaniment the mot skillful professional care, moral analysis and education will lack Christian authenticity.

Companionship (like sharing bread-table companionship) will only persist if the suffering is shared. This remark needs careful unpacking. Clearly one human person cannot fully understand the suffering of another and so share adequately even at the simply knowing level. Much less can person take over or share in a direct physical way another's pain. Yet sympathy and compassion are more than simple companionship or care. Indeed companionship and care are stimulated and sustained by the acceptance of the other in her suffering into one's heart and mind and imagination. Despite the limitations of language, we can say that we are sometimes inhabited by the others, by the suffering of the other. This compassionate reception of deprived human others is at the heart of Jesus' ministry. God's acceptance, being inhabited in Jesus by the burdens and pain, privations and failures (sins) of all human beings, is at the heart of the doctrine of salvation. In imitation of Jesus and of the Father disciples open themselves to the suffering others while respecting their distinctiveness as persons even in their suffering. The patronising encouragement of dependency fails to respect the suffering person from whom the carer has so much to receive. Companionship is at the service of the other's personal self-respect, integrity and autonomy. Compassionate companionship after the manner of Jesus and God, which involves co-creating, co-suffering and co-redeeming in the community of caring, may be the best description of the first moral obligation of disciples to people living with AIDS/HIV.

Care

To be true to itself compassionate companionship must seek to offer effective care to the suffering while encouraging and enabling them to care for themselves as far as possible. Given the limitations of their freedom, justice also demands such caring. Only in this way can they be integrated into the healing solidarity and peace of the kingdom. Care, like compassion and all other aspects of ministry, must constantly look for guidance to these primary kingdom values.

Care must operate at every level at which suffering operates and not be reduced simply to medical care, essential as that is. At the medical level itself the call to truth in researching further understanding of the origins, transmission and overcoming of the virus(es) has obvious kingdom resonances. A further kingdom call is to ensure that medical understanding is effectively disseminated, particularly where myths about origin and transmission are widespread. Sometimes these myths are simply due to ignorance. Sometimes they are promoted out of prejudice/prejudgement about so-called 'deviants' such as gay men or drug-users while information about heterosexual transmission is ignored or distorted.

Research into cause and cure is still so far from completion that it must be encouraged and funded as fully as possible. Meantime, the best medical care available must be provided as truthfully, as freely and as fairly or justly as possible. The manipulation of sufferers by deception or coercion in the name of treatment clearly violates personal dignity and kingdom values. Financial exploitation by medical and pharmaceutical interests is no less morally objectionable. Striving for fair distribution of therapies available becomes a particular Christian responsibility in a world where the powerful and privileged readily corner medical as well as other resources, and the generally deprived, especially in the third world, are exposed to the worst ravages of the disease.

Medical treatment, even much more effective treatment than is at present available, could not hope on its own to heal the psychological and social destruction wrought by AIDS/HIV. Counselling care remains critical to psychological healing. Social healing involves more radical measures from overcoming prejudice to cultural change to economic reform. Programmes of care in these different areas, which for Christians form part of the coming of the kingdom, will be effective only over time. The kingdom is coming, but in history only over time. This may be illustrated by one or two instances.

To care effectively for drug-users, already infected with HIV or exposed to infection, takes time. Drug-addiction is not cured instantly and by a simple decision of the will. Willingness to be helped will usually be very hard to elicit or to encourage. In the time needed for that an important first step in saving life and making time for recovery could be weaning people from the use of shared needles.

In the impoverished circumstances in which so many drug addicts live, it may be necessary, among other measures, to provide clean needles free of charge, without endorsing in any way drug-addiction or the drug-culture. A Christian care of drug-addicts, which seeks to protect the infected from infecting others, and the non-infected from being infected by others, could regard the provision of clean needles as a morally acceptable interim measure, where the interim is being used to save life and so offers some hope of tackling and eventually overcoming the drug-addiction and the drug-culture.

In quite different situations of AIDS/HIV transmission by sexual intercourse, prostitutes and their clients in sex-tourism and the sex industry may be no more capable of instant conversion than drug-addicts. This 'incapacity' has its psychological reason which vary with individual people. Social, cultural and economic reasons, which may be even stronger, vary with the particular society and culture. Some studies as well as popular impressions suggest that for prostitutes economic reasons may be strongest of all. To care for people with AIDS/HIV in these situations and as part of that care to prevent them spreading it further, every dimension of the problem has to be analysed and tackled. All this demands time for individual and groups. In that time care for life may require interim measures akin to the provision of clean needles for drug addicts. With all the risks of misunderstanding both in regard to the 'safety' of so-called safe sex and to the apparent of promiscuity, it may be socially necessary and morally legitimate to accept the use of condoms. However, it must be made clear that this is in no way regarded as good in itself. It is tolerated as an interim measure to protect life and allow time for the personal and social conversion which the coming of the kingdom calls for and enables in these situations also.

Casuistry

Discussion of care has already been involved analysis of typical cases or what has been more traditionally called casuistry. Despite its recent bad press among moral theologians and others, casuistry is a useful instrument in detailing Christian moral response to a range of difficulties. It must, however, be kept in its subordinate role of instrument and not be allowed to dominate Church moral discourses as it sometimes has in the past.

The approval, reluctantly, of needle exchange for drug-addicts infected or threatened by AIDS/HIV is an exercise in the ministry of casuistry. The general moral rejection of the use of these drugs is not in question. What is in question is now do you get this rejection to work for these people in a situation in which they are putting their own and other' lives at risk by sharing needles. To make time to set people free from the enslavement to drugs it is necessary to save them from the life threatening condition of AIDS/HIV. How far clean needles may help in the particular case is for the good case-worker and casuist to decide.

In further justification of such a decision the principle of lesser evil is invoked. It is morally right to seek to persuade somebody intent on evil to do a lesser evil. To wound rather than to kill where somebody is intent on shooting his neighbour to death. In just war discussion the principle of proportionality between the evil against which the war is waged and the evil the war is likely to involve has the same moral thrust. Just war theory recognises the inevitability of suffering and evil in war and calls for its reduction as far as possible.

The principle of the lesser evil has its limitations. In practice what counts as lesser? In theory can evil, however lesser, be properly intended and approved at all? The distinction between moral and pre-moral evil adopted by some recent moral theologians is sharply controverted by other moralists in situations like contraception and abortion for which it was first introduced. The principle of double effect suffers from much the same difficulties in similar situations.

A more general difficulty with the principle of lesser evil and variations on it might be its static view of the situation and there-fore its apparent surrender of moral principle for short-term and uncertain gain for person or community. In a more dynamic view of the situation the Christian and kingdom intent is to accompany and care for people beyond their present enslavement. With the goal of an eventual transformation of person, culture and commu-nity the first step to clean rather than dirty needles may be more easily seen as moral. It will be more easily seen of course by those engaged with the practice than by those elaborating the theory. And there may be more than one moral theory to support the prac-tice while no one theory may be entirely satisfactory. In life and in love, those major human and Christian realities, theory must fre-quently limp behind practice. This will return for consideration under the rubric of education.

A similar casuistic ministry could apply, as outlined above, to caring for people under threat from AIDS/HIV in certain sexual sit-uations. The moral growth into kingdom values has to start from where people are and everything morally possible must be done to help them survive into that period of growth. The concern over con-doms, which can become a fixation for some people, must be put in context. If their safety is falsely exaggerated by ignoring various potential sources of failure, human and mechanical, a more truthful approach is required. If condoms are introduced as a cover for endorsing promiscuity or exploiting the sex trade that should be exposed and opposed. Risks of this kind can never be entirely excluded and have to be balanced against the open and serious intention of liberating people from the danger to life into some hope of a humane and kingdom style of living. In this kind of situation the prohibition of *Humanae Vitae* on the use of artificial contracep-tives as disrupting the intrinsic connection between the unitive and procreative dimensions of the marriage act does not seem to apply. In these practices there is no truly unitive act to disrupt. Where a

married partner is infected the pressures created by AIDS/HIV on
the couple and their relationship would more readily persuade the
compassionate casuist that the use of condoms could be acceptable
to prevent an act of marital loving, which in the words of *Humane
Vitae* is divinely intended to be life-giving, from becoming death-
dealing.

Education

In preaching and teaching the good news of the kingdom the community of disciples is engaged in education. For that education to
be effective the community must practice what it preaches. The disciples' ministry of education must also be modelled on Jesus' ministry. Education or communication for conversion is based above all
on witness. In this light the ministries of companionship, of care
and of truthful and sensitive casuistry contain the heart of the
Church's education programme.

Education is also a two-way process. The would-be educators
must themselves be educated. The teachers must listen and learn.
With such a new phenomenon as AIDS/HIV and its continuing
developments only a learning Church can be an effective teaching
Church. A couple of implications of this rather obvious point may
be usefully spelled out.

Learning can and must take place at many different levels in the
Church and deal with many different aspects of the pandemic and
response to it. In this learning process persons living with
AIDS/HIV, their partners, companions and carers have much to
contribute. Through their experience they may have unique access
to understanding some of the moral needs and possibilities arising
out of the pandemic. This was adverted to earlier in the discussion
of casuistry. The interaction between this immediate experience
and associated understanding and the moral tradition of the
Church may already be yielding results. This, however, takes time
and no theological or theoretical analysis may be entirely adequate
to the practical experience and understanding. Mutual education
between the practising and the teaching Church must continue.
And there are more serious issues pending than the couple of examples cited earlier might indicate.

Pastoral modification of the kind suggested by the discussion of
drug addiction and sexual intercourse in the context of AIDS/HIV
do not seriously affect traditional Catholic positions. The rereading
they imply is not really revisionary. Yet as already mentioned there
are gaps in the Catholic moral theology of sexuality. It has little pos-

itive to say about sexual morality outside marriage. In an area where experience should count in discernment and formulation women's experience has scarcely been heard. The need for development then is not simply occasioned by the spread of AIDS/HIV.

Catholic moral teaching on sexuality, while it has a solid central core in regard to marriage, may have a good deal to learn about the wider meaning if it is to provide adequate education to future generations. One area in which many people with AIDS/HIV, their companions and carers are struggling is that of homosexuality. Part of the struggle and suffering is caused by prejudice and social rejection. The Christian call to unconditional acceptance of all people and especially of the marginalised must clearly apply to homosexuals as people. It cannot be achieved overnight. Education is needed. That education will have to face new evidence about the origins and development of homosexuality. Kingdom truth demands no less, and the kingdom values of justice and freedom exclude discrimination against homosexuals just as much as against other social 'lepers'. The kingdom value of peace with its implications of unity, reconciliation and forgiveness confirms this need to integrate homosexuals into a genuinely Christian and inclusive community.

What further shifts in attitude and practice new evidence and reconsideration of old positions require is far from clear. That homosexual orientation is no longer regarded as a matter of self-indulgence or personal whim would seem reasonable. Beyond that the witness of remarkable loving care which some gay men show to their partners and friends with AIDS/HIV should be recognised as of moral and Christian significance. The moral superiority of stable relationships between homosexual males as compared with casual relationships can hardly be denied. Such education which is coming mainly from the front-lines of the AIDS/HIV crisis has yet to interact effectively with the directors of Catholic education. What the outcome of that interaction will be cannot be predicted here. Meantime, the companions and carers must act as lovingly as they can on the basis of the best insights available to them.

Continuing the story

Theology remains permanently unfinished. The stories, the caring and the grieving, tragic and inspiring, continue; so must the theological reflection. And for all the suffering and the threat posed to the whole human community, the stories may also open up fresh possibilities of redemption and liberation by the inbreaking kingdom of God.

CHAPTER 12

Human identities and reconciliation

Identity, personal and communal

Identity questions are many and complex. Identity answers few and inadequate. The multiplicity of the questions and the inadequacy of the answers inevitably increase as one moves from personal identity to communal identity. Person and community are intimately related and so are their identities. For most inquirers, however, community or group identity displays such a range of variables that its description tends to become abstract and vague, or if more concrete, simple and reductionist. Stereotypes of black people or Irish as stupid, or of women as the weaker sex, illustrate the reductionist strategy.

Universal versus particular

In many disciplines and discourses today there are two conflicting trends which apply to the discussion of human identity relevant here. The universalising trend, a legacy in its present form of the European Enlightenment, sees human identity in terms of membership of the whole human race. Human identity is, in this sense, universal, shared by all the human inhabitants of planet earth. It distinguishes human beings from other inhabitants of the earth, animate and inanimate, animals, birds, fish, plants, rocks, mountains and rivers. And it distinguishes them from possible inhabitants of other planets or galaxies, Martians or aliens from space. The continuities and connections of humans and other terrestrials (or extra-terrestrials) may qualify but do not, in most minds and practices, eliminate the distinctiveness of the human being. This common human identity is expressed and reinforced by technological advances in communication and travel and by economic, cultural, moral and even religious exchanges. Not all of this is enriching in any human terms but it provides a powerful indicator of the shared humanity of the exchangers.

This 'Modern' tendency, as it is sometimes called, may be set against a 'Post-modern' in which the emphasis is on the particularity of human individuals, and more especially of human groups and their stories. The terminology 'modern' and 'post-modern' is not especially illuminating but it helps place this discussion in a wider if untidy context. The emphasis on particular group identities emerged very clearly after World War II in the worldwide process of decolonisation. This marked the end of empire, European empire for much of Asia and Africa. Particular peoples, for so long integrated into empire, began to assert their own identities as peoples and to seek to express them in political aspirations and structures. This did not prove easy in the seeking or achieving. The colonial legacy frequently involved a mismatch between established political boundaries and existing ethnic and cultural particularities. The hostile and sometimes lethal divisions which have afflicted so many countries in Asia and Africa are part of this legacy.

Meantime another empire was developing in Eastern Europe and Asia, the Soviet Empire, with its universal claims and oppressive system. Its collapse in recent years has seen the emergence of old particularities with renewed and destructive enmities. Group identity, ethnic, cultural and religious, has become a badge of difference, of competitive and frequently destructive difference, of which the most powerful symbol has been 'ethnic cleansing'. In a world in which a United Nations organisation struggles to provide a unified forum for the resolution of conflict, in which a Declaration of Human Rights is accepted in principle by all, in which world trade, travel and communications imply a fair degree of universal human community and identity, particularities and differences of identity continue on their destructive ways.

This perspective, with its apparent bias towards the value of a universal human identity as against the dangers of strong particular group identities, is European in thought and language. It has its own concealed particularity which, in various forms, has sought to dominate the rest of the world. This comment is not intended to deny the value, indeed the enduring value, of much of this European and implicitly Christian achievement. However, it is necessary to alert European philosophers and theologians, political and religious leaders, to the particularities of their own version of universality and to its inherent temptations to imperialism. Alertness to the dangers, and allowance for the biases, helps the European to contribute positively to the world conversation on human identity, universal and particular.

A further twist on the road to understanding human identity in its continuities and discontinuities has been preoccupying environmentalists and ecologists. Speciesism is a recent addition to the sins attributed to humankind. On the more positive side the interconnection of all planetary and eventually cosmic realities has located humanity as one species which must live in interdependence on the planet. Anthropocentrism, or human domination or exploitation of other living species, is no more acceptable than white people's domination of black or men's of women. Indeed women are among the leading thinkers and activists in contextualising human beings within the earth's environment. Eco-feminism is making its own contribution to defining human identity, with its emphasis on the interconnectedness of everything. The fall of a butterfly in Calcutta, as the saying goes, can influence a tornado in the Caribbean. All this exposes new levels of particularity and universality, with the stress on the connectedness and unity still seeking a balance between the particular or the individual and the universal or community.

Persons in community: Communities of persons

Back at the human level of identity, the communal dimensions of personal identity and the personal dimensions of communal identity require further elaboration. Persons become persons only in communities; communities are composed of persons. This is evident in the family where children come into existence and grow into personhood first of all by the procreative power of their father and mother, and develop personally through their relationships with their parents, their siblings, their friends and peers, their neighbours and the local community. From these they receive their biological endowment, their language, culture and religion, as they become in turn contributors to the overlapping communities to which they belong. Out of the community inheritance, and in a series of relationships, they gradually fashion their individual personal identity. For all its personal distinctiveness which self and others come to recognise, that personal identity remains communal through and through. Particular persons are always persons in and of a community, even when they change or reject community. Desert hermits like Anthony, and creative, rejecting geniuses like James Joyce, could not escape their biological, cultural or religious inheritance as their lives and writings show.

In parallel fashion, true communities are communities of persons. In his freshly influential work, 'Moral Man and Immoral

Society', American theologian Reinhold Niebuhr argued that the person was bound by, and could fulfil, a more stringent set of moral principles than any society or community could. Biblical morality was a morality of the person; looser moral demands rested on society and politics. True communities and societies were not expected to match the true person in moral attainment. The argument as a whole is for another forum. Here it suffices to note Niebuhr's insistence that there are moral standards to be upheld by society and that they are about the protection and promotion of persons, the generally accepted moral position in the west for many centuries. True or moral communities must respect persons and personhood. This is the basic meaning of justice. Where this justice is violated on a large scale, the society or community is no longer truly human. It surrenders its human identity. We have not lacked horrible examples of such inhuman societies in Europe in this century. Some are still with us, others not far away.

The inhuman societies which dominate our memories and imaginations are the tyrannical societies of Hitler and Stalin and their imitators. In recent decades, inhumanity has flourished in the collectivist oppression of would-be Marxist societies like the USSR where the individual was deprived of personal rights and personal life in the name of the collective, of the people. The collapse of such oppressive regimes had to be warmly welcomed. Only thus could personal and group identities be recognised and realised again. The ensuing difficulties for persons and groups in Eastern Europe and elsewhere referred to earlier, do not devalue the liberating achievement of the collapse of the communist regimes. However, they highlight a weakness which western and anti-communist countries tended to ignore in themselves, their difficulty in developing true community in liberal, democratic capitalist societies. This weakness may have been most obvious in the 1980s under the influence of Margaret Thatcher in Britain and Ronald Reagan in the USA. It was summarised in Thatcher's crude declaration to the Assembly of the Church of Scotland, 'There is no such thing as society', only individuals – competing. In their jurisdictions, many could not compete on the terms laid down; individuals with their identities and dignified life-styles were lost; only the strongest flourished. True community and true personal identity were sorely diminished.

The person as plural
In examining further human identity in person and community, the

multiplicity and complexity of inheritance and of current and developing relationships, may be more fruitfully understood if the person and not only the community is considered as plural. Indeed the person may be seen as a community itself, in the convergence of ancestral influences, personal experiences and relationships as well as of broader historical and social forces. Genealogies in the Bible and in current western fashion are a search for identity through the ancestral and communal inheritance. In personal experiences and relationships, identity is developed by the integration, conscious and unconscious, of friends and enemies, of triumphs and failures. Broader historical and social forces exercise their influence right through each human life.

In concrete terms, Patrick Murphy of Cork is son and grandson of parents and grandparents who leave their genetic, psychological, political and religious mark. His identity as Murphy, Cork, Irish and Catholic is already complex and multiple. In the course of his life it develops and changes in multiple ways. He migrates to Dublin or London to work, where he becomes part of a new city or even country, where he marries and his children grow up to influence him too with quite different generational relationships. His community of influences and interests is changing. He is becoming a new community, a new and fragile coalition of differing *personae*. He has always been such, like all his fellow citizens and fellow Catholics. Irish people are part of western culture but with their own distinctive features. They are deeply intertwined with their largest neighbour, Britain. Irish identity includes in all Irish people important British elements, above all the English language. The intractability of British-Irish political relations, as embodied in the troubles in Northern Ireland, derives from the complexity of Irish identity, north and south. Even the apparently simpler distinction of Protestant and Catholic is misleading. Irish Catholics, like other Northern European Catholics, are inheritors of the Reformation-Counter Reformation disputes and wars. So are Irish and European Protestants. Neither side can be identified theologically, psychologically or politically independently of the other.

They inhabit each other in what in the past have been taken to be hostile ways but today should be seen as mutually correcting and enriching. Cork's original Paddy Murphy emerges as plural, incorporating rich and diverse dimensions which enable him to connect more directly and fruitfully with quite different others with whom he, as community-person, has much more in common than perhaps he ever realised. In the Irish context it would be important for him to recognise how much he has in common with Sammy Thompson of Belfast, Protestant and Unionist. To enable Paddy and Sammy to recognise their common gifts in the present estrangement is a daunting task. Recognition of each one's identity as plural is a necessary beginning.

Others and strangers in community

In considering the person as plural, attention had to be paid to the different, the other. Irish and British, Catholic and Protestant are, for most people like Paddy Murphy and Sammy Thompson, different and other in opposition. In the plural person the different coalesce, the other belongs somehow in the self. This paradox is sharpened if the other is spoken of as the stranger, a more sinister and potentially hostile word. The paradox is more acceptable in a community of persons than in a person conceived as a community.

Human differentiation as persons involves an irreducible otherness, in the sense that one person may not and eventually cannot possess, dispose of or manipulate another person as he might an object. The person as other always finally transcends every other person. This inability to control the other often makes the other into a threat. Familial, civil and ecclesiastical politics frequently confirm this. More profoundly, the other comes as gift. The ambiguity between gift and threat leads to misunderstanding, hostility and even war. Enabling the gift of the other to triumph over the threat is the task of community formers and leaders. It is the meaning of reconciliation. For Christians, it is what Jesus accomplishes in his life and ministry, in his death and resurrection.

Otherness and strangeness are basically and finally sources of enrichment, essential to the formation of real community. From Northern Ireland to Bosnia to Sri Lanka to Peru, the otherness and strangeness have for so long been sources of hostile and even murderous division. And they are only a few instances of what appears to be humanity's prevailing disease, the perception and treatment of the stranger as threat.

From many points of view, this is a question of identity of person and community. Indeed, it is a question of mistaken identity. The presenting mistake is that of seeing the other as primarily threat instead of recognising him as potential gift. The further mistaken identity is one of the self, by excluding, out of fear perhaps, the elements of the other which enter into one's own identity as community or person. When Paddy Murphy of Cork and Sammy Thompson of Belfast come to recognise their own plural identities, and how they overlap in diverse ways, even at points where they seem most opposed, their larger communities will begin to recognise their larger identities in a relationship of justice. Otherness and strangeness will then become the true basis for reconciliation in community, for mutual respect and acceptance as gift to one another.

CHAPTER 13

God as stranger in ethics
A European perspective

The naming of a discipline

In English, as in many other languages, ethics is used in a number of related senses. Basically there are two such senses, that of ethics as describing or prescribing the moral behaviour of individuals or groups, and that of ethics as an academic discipline or discourse. In another context it would be important to distinguish descriptive and prescriptive. Indeed the separating out of the academic cannot always be followed through even in academe, as it needs the continuous critique of actual practice. For Christians and theologians there are further complications. This relation between Christian faith and ethics has been interpreted in different ways within the Christian tradition itself. The Reformation and Counter-Reformation debate resulted in two very different titles for the academic discipline, *Christian Ethics* and *Moral Theology*. And some Reform theologians added or preferred the title *Practical Theology*. In method, emphasis and detailed conclusion, these two traditions of ethics for Christians could differ sharply. Obvious differences in the quite recent past centred on the roles of the Bible, natural law and church authority. These are still matters of debate, but within as well as between the traditions.

The difficulty of naming arises here to illustrate the complexity of the task set: 'God as stranger in ethics'. In the European context as well as in its Christian theological context, 'ethics' is a very fluid concept and practice. The author's background in moral theology and as a Catholic priest affects the choices and the necessary simplifications to be made. In many ways, however, this will be more of a personal meditation than an academic exercise. The practice of theology must often nowadays move beyond the strictly academic, while taking due account of it, to the more imaginative and meditative. There are dangers in this approach, dangers of not taking the tradition or its best analysts seriously enough, dangers of self-indulgence and superficiality. In confronting and perhaps partially overcoming them, the meditative exercise can be purified and deepened and the risk proved worthwhile.

Ethics as the practice and discourse of exclusion

One of the proud boasts of western and Christian ethics in the modern period would surely be its universalism. It applies to all people equally. The United Nations Declaration of Human Rights is fruit and symbol of this vision and vehicle for its implementation. While there may be a historical case, it seems perverse to describe ethics today as the practice and discourse of exclusion. That father of western ethics, Aristotle, now coming into favour again, developed a clearly exclusivist ethics from and for the behaviour of the free men of Athens. In this he was not alone among the ancient philosophers. Religious, racial and male exclusivism characterised much of the ethical practice and understanding of that other fountainhead of western ethics, the Hebrew tradition. The Christian tradition itself was marked by these inheritances. Theological giants such as Augustine and Aquinas could not entirely transcend these exclusivist limitations, as women or Jews or Donatists might bear witness. Medieval crusades, destruction of indigenous peoples in the 'New World', and religious wars in the sixteenth and seventeenth centuries with their theological justification, kept the tradition of exclusivist ethics alive and well and blessed by the imperial God of Europe, Catholic or Protestant.

The Enlightenment would have ended all that religious, politic and racial particularity in ethical thought and practice. Kant's rule of universalisability, and the American and French insistence on the rights of man, would ensure an inclusive ethics with equality of treatment and respect for all. Liberalism in economics and politics was the only sure way to guarantee the end of exclusion and destruction. Black American slaves would find that hard to believe; the native American peoples would find it even harder, presuming they lived long enough to hear of it. So would Irish and other European famine victims. The new European scramble for Africa in the second half of the nineteenth century was not obviously enlightened or inclusive in its ethical practice either. All these exclusionist practices had their enlightened and liberal justifiers. The great Irish Famine was a typical instance in which racial and religious prejudice combined with liberal theory to resist government interference and let freedom and death prevail.

For all its pretensions to ethical superiority, twentieth century Europe has been extraordinarily exclusivist and destructive. Its powerful reactions to the limitations of liberal individualism in Nazism and Soviet Communism exposed frightening new dimensions of human destructiveness. The Jewish Holocaust and the Stalinist purges stand out in a Europe immersed in two self-inflicted great wars. Philosophers, theologians and ethicists, religious and secular, had their own part in preparing and justifying many of these horrors. And the horrors are not over yet, as Bosnia illustrates.

Less obvious in a Europe struggling to establish some kind of peaceful unity of the traditional nations are the continuing economic and racial exclusions. In most European countries the gap between rich and poor is getting wider while the European Union itself behaves as another rich and exclusive club in relation to the poorer countries of the developing world. The ethics of the free market and of world trade is neatly adjusted to preserving the privileges of the richer western countries.

To complete the prosecution case against the practice and theory of European ethics as exclusivist, is the traditional treatment of women. Much has undoubtedly changed in practice in recent decades in some countries. Yet the language and preoccupation of the major ethical theoretical debates reflect very little of women's experience and oppression. Indeed some of the most critical practical debates on issues such as abortion and war are, in theology at least, frequently conducted without reference to any special contribution women might make. In accusing European ethics of exclusivism, its historic exclusion of women from ethical discourse proves a telling point.

This reading of western and Christian ethics or moral theology as practice and discourse of exclusion, itself excludes other more inclusivist strands in the whole tradition. And these will play their part later. The strengths of the exclusions are seldom given sufficient attention, or may become matters of dispute within the tradition while not seen as affecting the whole. In the context of this essay, it is important to recognise how easily ethics may be captive to a particular culture and interest and exclude, perhaps unconsciously, as foreign or strange or other to its concerns, a range of human beings and interests. These human strangers are the first casualties of so many ethical systems and practices. God as stranger in ethics is inevitably related in practice and theory to these human strangers or others.

Inclusivist strands in western ethics

As already indicated, more inclusivist strands exist within the western tradition of ethics, both religious and secular, practical and theoretical. The prophetic tradition of Amos, for example, sharply criticises the exclusivist practices of the wealthy and powerful in face of the poor, the widows and orphans and the strangers. The major Hebrew prophets offer similar critique. Care of the marginalised within Israel, and hospitality to the stranger from without, is a persistent if not always dominant theme of the Hebrew scriptures. The rediscovery of Jesus as prophet in this tradition, and the emphasis in his ministry and teaching on the poor and excluded, has refocussed theology in new ways exemplified in Latin America and other Third World theologies and in feminist and similar theologies in the developed world. Of course these concerns were never simply lost to Europe but they seldom played a formative role in systematic thinking about ethics.

In more recent secular developments, there was clearly a prophetic and inclusivist role in both liberal and socialist thought and action. The equality and rights language of the eighteenth century initiated a movement of liberation and inclusion which is still to be completed. The counter-example of the French Terror cannot obscure that, anymore than the Gulags of the Soviets can wipe out the prophetic and economically inclusive thrusts of early Marxism. To dismiss these insights or ideals now, or the achievements in personal freedoms and social justice they have prompted for so many, would be clearly unfair. Just as it would be unfair to ignore the serious limitations listed earlier and the exclusions they promoted and still project. In his encyclical, *Sollicitudo Rei Socialis,* Pope John Paul II offered a balanced ethical critique of the economic dimensions of the liberal and socialist traditions. The balanced historical view might seek to maintain, in some kind of tension, the inclusivist and exclusivist tendencies in the various ethical traditions and practices. Such effort would be valuable and justified, particularly given the present 'post-modern' tendency to rush to extreme judgement in attack on or in defence of versions of liberalism, socialism, communitarianism, republicanism, Aristotelianism and even Thomism, among others. The focus of this essay is different, not on historical balancing but on exploration of the apparent source of exclusion, the reality and concept of the stranger, the other.

Human otherness in an inclusive ethics

The 'insider' character of most ethical traditions was part of their social and historical development. A historical community, however loosely defined, had its own moral ideals and practices which applied, in the first instance and fullest sense, to the dominant group in the community, free men or members of the tribe or particular religious believers. Women or heretics or slaves or strangers did not enjoy the same moral claims or responsibilities. They were other than the defining group. That otherness was often a matter of degree, women could have more claims than slaves, slaves than heretics or strangers. And there was room for further development. Slavery was, after all, finally abolished in the western world although its consequences linger in racial discrimination or exclusion. The women's liberation movement is still far from achieving moral and legal parity. Any claim to an inclusive ethic by westerners or Christians or any other group continues to be undermined by the structures, practices and justifications of exclusion and marginalisation. Some others are just too other or strange to be truly and fully included.

What is missing in this analysis is the recognition that moral claim and responsibility, while it always occurs within a community and shared tradition, is equally dependent on the otherness within that community. It is recognition of, respect for and response to the human other, as other, that is at the heart of western and Christian morality. Such recognition, respect and response have a historical genesis within particular communities. Otherness or strangeness or difference in community has given its dynamism to moral behaviour and moral theory.

Otherness, strangeness and difference are used here interchangeably. Qualifications may be needed later as the argument develops and moves beyond human otherness to the otherness of God. The core claim here is that it is the presence of human others, in their otherness and in community, however vague, which establishes moral relationship. And this applies in varying modes and degrees along the western moral tradition. In so far as that tradition practised and justified exclusion, it was obscuring and perhaps falsifying a central feature of itself. Another human being or human group, whose humanity is recognised and therefore recognised as shared and as other, may be a rather awkward way of describing the origins and structure of moral relationship. The extent of the recognition of the human otherness of the others has determined the extent of their full moral status and of their inclusion or exclusion in a particular moral world. The brief reference to the history of moral exclusion rests on the varying degrees of human otherness attributed to slaves, children, women, blacks, native Americans, gays etc. This degree of otherness can change over time, for children becoming adults, for various groups and nations achieving emancipation. The history of human emancipation and moral equality is one of differentiation in communion. Gender or class or race are recognised and respected in their full human otherness within an extended, inclusive and equal human community. The scope of the inclusive ethical community is both particular and universal, embracing the differentiation of all human beings, their communities and cultures, living and participating equally in communion.

Human otherness and divine

The term *otherness* has strong historical roots as well as valuable contemporary connections. In the Hebrew scriptures the 'holy', as applied to the God of the covenant and associated places and events, derived from *qadosh* which meant separated or other. The much later usage of ultimate other for God carried these Hebrew overtones of holiness and transcendence. In moral terms, the people were covenanted to God and one another. Worship was intrinsically related to morality, to treatment of the neighbour and particularly to that of the poor neighbour and excluded neighbour, the widow, the orphan, the stranger. (Amos, Isaiah, *et al*). The justice and righteousness of God, which characterised his response to his people, must characterise their response to one another and, in this, preference must be given to the deprived or excluded. For Jeremiah this response to the excluded, to do justice, is to know God. The transcendent otherness of God entering into covenant communion with the people of Israel requires that communion of others within Israel itself and with particular attention to the usually excluded and the stranger. The translation from divine to human was never complete within Israel, but the dynamic was there. That dynamic picked up the more universal concerns of the God of creation in their reaching out to all human and indeed all created otherness. The new covenant would introduce the new creation and the new communion or *koinonia*.

In Jesus' ministry, the new thing promised by the prophets was accomplished. The inclusivity of his ministry within Israel, with priority given to the poor, sinners, women, prepared his disciples for the inclusivity which they were to preach and practice in the new community of the good news. A critical feature of this preaching and practice was forgiveness of sin, reconciliation between God and human beings, and between human beings themselves. 'Who can forgive sins except God alone?' 'Go in peace, your sins are forgiven you.' 'Father forgive them for they know not what they do.' 'Forgive us our trespasses as we forgive those who trespass against us.' 'If you come to the altar and there remember that your brother has anything against you, go first and be reconciled with your brother.' 'If anyone is in Christ he is a new creation; the old has passed away, behold, the new has come. All this is from God, who through Christ reconciled us to himself and gave us the ministry of reconciliation; that is, God was in Christ reconciling the world to himself' (1 Cor 5:17-19).

The return of Israel and humanity to community in reconciliation with God and one another, which is central to the message and mission of Hebrew prophets and their successor Jesus, constitutes a critical call to inclusivity. This must be the ethics of accepting the others as others, forgiving them and integrating with them. The New Testament words for reconciliation, *diaallassein* and *kataallassein*, means bringing those who are other (*allos*) into community. For that, in Judeo-Christian terms, the reconciling presence and power of God is necessary. The new reign of God must come as for Christians it did in Jesus Christ. In the horizon the stories of Israel and of Jesus' human otherness, based eventually on the image of divine otherness, can only become authentic and fulfiled in communion. Gross individualism or oppressive collectivism or communitarianism are destructive of both human otherness and true community. A genuinely inclusive ethics is possible through deeper differentiation of others in fuller communion. For Christians, this remains both gift and task within history; the already under pressure from the not yet.

Traditions in interaction

The Jewish and Christian traditions have always developed in interaction with wider worlds of ideas and practices, religious, philosophical, political and economic. This is particularly true of moral understanding and living. Otherness and community as they emerged in Judaism and Christianity have their parallels and influence in these wider worlds. For all its inclusivity Aristotle's treatment of ethics and particularly of justice provided a starting point for recognising the otherness of the free man as the other, who must be respected and responded in his independent equality. Intervening philosophical and political traditions conserved some of this equality in otherness and otherness in communion. The medieval recovery of Aristotle and his integration, particularly by Aquinas, into Christian theology confirmed, criticised and developed some of the Aristotelian ideas in the light of Christian thinking.

For Aquinas, justice is basically concerned with the (human) other (*ad alterum*). The degree of otherness determines the kind and degree of Justice. So wives in relation to husbands, or children in relation to parents, or subjects in relation to political authorities, are not fully other and so do not enjoy exact equality or strict justice in their relations. In Aquinas, religion is affiliated to justice as its cardinal virtue. The due which much be paid to everybody, in Aquinas' concept of justice, must be paid to God also. The divine otherness demands its own recognition and respect.

In recent philosophy, literature and the arts the other as outsider and stranger has played a significant role, from Camus to Levinas to various 'post-modernists'. In theology some of this influence from theology and literature is evident. Levinas is one obvious example. Theologians themselves, in face of the horrific exclusions and annihilations of the twentieth century and of theology's own exclusion from much intellectual, political and other discourse, have developed their own theologies of the excluded and marginalised, of the other, in liberation, black, feminist and similar theologies. These theologies, as indicated above, have not greatly influenced western moral theology or Christian ethics, still less western ethics *tout court*. It is the contention of this chapter that the recovery of the other/stranger, human and divine, is at the heart of the renewal of ethics and of God's proper place within it.

Strange gods and the stranger God

The differentiation in some community, which the recognition of the other/stranger implies, has its own shadow side. Indeed stranger, as the history of exclusion shows, may present more as threat, as potentially destructive than as gift and potentially enriching. This ambiguity affects all human relationships from the most intimate within the family to the most structured in economic, cultural and political life. Children may be seen predominantly and persistently as threat to the well-being or comfort of parents. The threat dimension which the fetal other has assumed for many today, with its fatal consequences, provides a striking example of fear of the other. Letting the gift triumph over the threat, the welcome and acceptance over the fear and distrust, is a way of describing a human ethics that is nourished by the Jewish Christian story, but is open to other stories, other cultures and other peoples.

That continuing openness derives for Christians from their stories of an ultimate other as manifested in stories of creation, of Israel, of Jesus and of disciples who saw in the hungry stranger a further manifestation of the Stranger God. The return of the stranger to ethical theory and practice prepares the way not only for the excluded humans but also for the excluded creator and, indeed, for the hitherto excluded non-human creation. The recurring attempts to establish a purely anthropocentric ethics become readily exclusivist in gender, class or race. The threat which the ultimate other may pose is sidestepped or ignored, while some other godling assumes centre-stage. The strange impoverished gods of money or power or pleasure become refuges from the real, disturbing and stranger God. By facing up to the judging and subversive, but finally loving and transforming presence and power of the Stranger God, the strange gods can be finally banished.

Many of the current or recent debates about a purely human ethics, or a specifically Christian ethics, or more recently about an ethics of the environment, have been misconceived. The simple universality and rationality sometimes invoked, ignored both the historical character of all human reasoning, the rich diversity of other traditions and the shadow side of all human otherness. Evil or sin do not figure except as aberrations in much moral discourse. The Stranger God of the marginalised and the crucified, which Christians bring with them to the debates, could promote a much more hospitable context for discourse. The Stranger God of the creation stories of Genesis and Job and so on, help to appreciate the otherness of all creatures and creation in their primarily enriching, but at least occasionally threatening, potential.

The strangeness of God, which is strewn all over creation and the history of salvation, has still further dimensions for Christians. What emerges in their experience of Jesus and his achievement is not only an otherness or strangeness of God but an otherness or strangeness within God in the perfect inclusivity of the Trinity. This otherness in communion is source and culmination of creation's striving, the eschatological completion of the moral life in a new creation, when exclusivism will be finally excluded and all creation will enjoy the differentiation in communion which properly and fully belongs to our Stranger God.

CHAPTER 14

Fruit of the earth – work of human hands

In the renewal of sacramental life and understanding, Catholic cent-rality of the eucharist has appeared to survive intact. In the words of Augustine Birrell from his days at First Secretary in Ireland, 'It is still the Mass that matters'. It certainly matters in official exhorta-tion and theological reflection, as it matters to millions of ordinary Sunday and daily Mass-goers. The millions of Catholics who never or rarely attend Mass either through choice or necessity must qualify the easy assumption of centrality. Where their lack of attendance is necessitated by shortage of male celibate priests, the official emphasis on the centrality of the eucharist must also be qualified. A particular model of ordained priesthood may be treated as more important in practice than providing the priestly people with the opportunity to celebrate eucharist.

The eucharist as centre of the church's sacraments (Aquinas, *et al*) and of the church as sacrament (Rahner, Schillebeeckx, *et al*) has dominated much of the Catholic theological discussion. The ecu-menical discussion has sought to integrate these insights with the concerns of the Reformed and Orthodox Churches in a variety of ways. The parameters of these discussions within and between churches have been ecclesial and salvific. Redemption and salva-tion, sacrifice and meal, presence and symbol, have been the cur-rency of what has been really an in-house debate of the *domus Dei* (*Jesu Christi*). In an increasingly post-Christian and, however one interprets it exactly, post-modern context, such debate may appear marginal, eccentric rather than central. In a world threatened by human destructiveness militarily and ecologically, agreed state-ments on the eucharist, and even the developments of inter-church celebration, may appear trivial and peripheral. The formal *domus Dei* must lift its eyes to the gifts and needs of the whole world about it, the *mundus Dei*, if it would truly worship God. For this God is the God of creation as well as redemption. Church and sacraments, eucharist supreme among them, must recover their role as *sacramenta mundi*, effective symbols of the divine creative and redemptive activity which cannot be separated into any two-tiered system of sacred and secular. Indeed the fundamental unity of the divine work in creation and redemption is essential to understanding the meaning and centrality of eucharist for Catholics and all Christians. Only in this setting can the relevance and effectiveness of the eucharist be maintained and the sacredness, or better, the sacramentality of all creation, cosmic and human, be rediscovered.

Worship and morality

The unity of creation and redemption applies in a particularly powerful way to the ethical concerns of this chapter.

Worship and morality are intimately linked in the Jewish-Christian tradition. Herein lies the distinctiveness of ethics for Christians, that worship and morality constitute two sides of the one human response to Creator/Redeemer and to creation/redeemed. The core of the Catholic tradition of morality, in its natural law form, depends not primarily on Stoic concepts but on a theology of creation/new creation. The intrinsic and intimate connection between mysticism and morality was finally established in Jesus Christ as 'the way, the truth and the life' (Jn 14:6).

Word and sacrament, while distinct and yet united in Christ and church, can be functionally separated in misleading ways. The Reform emphasis on the word has been historically opposed to the Catholic emphasis on sacrament. In the older tradition, sacrament could not exist without word and the primary expressions of the word were in Jesus, in the believing community and in the eucharist. Vatican II and ecumenical dialogue have helped to restore this earlier unity and to renew word for Catholics and sacrament for Reformed ... to a certain extent. A rather different but related opposition has emerged with the development of recent prophetic theologies. Liberation theologies of diverse forms, Latin American, black and feminist, have seen themselves as primarily theologies of the word. Sacrament fits less easily on to their biblical basis and their political thrust towards radical reform. Indeed actual sacramental practice may be interpreted as endorsing the political *status quo* and opposed to the liberation and justice sought by the liberationists. In fidelity to their prophetic predecessors in Hebrew tradition and in Jesus, these theologians challenge such sacramental worship as idolatry or magic. The worship of idols, of the false gods of power or money, is the continuing temptation of the powerful and their courtly priests. For the powerless, the temptations of magical healing and liberation in place of human analysis and struggle may also co-opt the sacraments to the service of oppression. It is one of the aims of this chapter to expose the prophetic role of the eucharist and so reinforce the unity in difference of word and sacrament.

Fruit of the earth

As fruit of the earth, the bread and wine of the eucharist are rooted in creation, in planet and in cosmos. The cosmic story, from the theoretical 'Big Bang' to human consciousness and creativity, is traceable in flashback through the elementary and yet highly sophisticated elements of human food and drink employed by Jesus and the church in the eucharist. The Creator Spirit drew out of the void and lured into increasingly complex existence, the world we acknowledge but have scarcely begun to explore and understand. Despite enormous advances the elusive fundamental particles are more mysterious to contemporary scientists than atoms were to Democritus or protons and electrons to Niels Bohr. And while astronomy and cosmology continue to thrive and to make headlines for lay as well as scientific observers, concepts like 'Big Bang' and 'expanding universe' excite and delight without providing rounded explanation. The list could go on indefinitely. Sciences of matter and mind, in their unceasing progress, illuminate more and more without necessarily explaining. The growing light they shed emphasises the larger darkness of origins and purpose, of creativity and freedom, of failure and death. In all this they at once resemble and complement artists, whose insights and creations derive from other angles of vision and other designs of nature. Artistic sense of limit and mystery may resemble that of religion more than that of science. Yet, in the religious world of sacrament, the discoveries of science and the insights of art can enrich theological attempts to relate sacraments, especially eucharist, to creation and creativity.

The otherness of creation to Creator, a central mystery for Christians and all believers, is the basis of God's respect for creation. In Genesis terms, God saw that it was good. God regarded it in its goodness, recognised and respected it as valuable and to be valued. The Creator maintained a communion of respect and care for creation. As God's self-expression made other, creation shares the sacredness of God while being utterly different. Difference in community characterises the Creator-creation relationship, although the precise nature of the difference and of the communion will always elude human comprehension.

As creation is respected in its otherness by God, by its very otherness it at once reflects and respects God. By being itself, creation
acknowledges its Creator; it implicitly worships God. The developing
world of Genesis and of contemporary science, for all their differences, proclaim still more the glory of God. The growing differentiation within the world has, over the millennia, exposed more deeply
its otherness from God and, at the same time, manifested more fully
the inexhaustible riches of God. God's caring regard for this
increasing differentiation, leading to life and human life, has
received biblical recognition from Genesis to Job to Jesus. 'Behold
the lilies of the field ...' (Mt 6:28).

Bread and wine as fruit of the earth share in the divine respect
for all creation. In the symbolic world of the eucharist, they represent earth and its highly differentiated forms of life and nurture.
The divine regard for such life and nurture entered a new phase
with Jesus' blessing of the bread and wine, and his giving them to
eat and drink as his body and blood. For those who would eat and
drink worthily the body and blood of the Lord, the divine regard
for earth and its fruits represented by the bread and wine must also
receive human expression. Degrading and exploiting the earth with
its millions of life forms is to ignore the model of divine respect and
to insult the divine gift. Eucharist as recognition and celebration of
creation as well as redemption provides the basis and the seal of an
ecological ethics. The sacred character of the earth is confirmed in
the sacramental elements of the eucharist. All bread and wine is
now seen to be holy and to be respected as such. So is the ground on
which we walk. Failure to recognise and live that eucharistic understanding of earth and its gifts is failure to recognise the divine giver
also.

Work of human hands

All human work presupposes the divine labour of creation. With
the emergence of human creativity, true collaboration with the creative work of God became possible. Human development of the
world of creation becomes co-creation with the Creator God. In that
co-operation between divine and human creativity, the farming
and cooking revolutions led to the development of bread and wine,
two of the greatest achievements of divine-human collaboration.
The original divine labour of creation and the subsequent divine-
human collaboration form essential preparation for the integration
of bread and wine, eating and drinking, into the great liturgical act
of the eucharist. The divine labour of creation and the human work

of co-creation together make up the *praeparatio liturgica* of Christian worship and in particular of the eucharist. Invitation to the celebration of eucharist implies invitation to join the *praeparatio*. Inclusion in the eucharistic celebration should mean inclusion in the work of human hands.

Exclusion from human work is a widespread and depressing feature of our civilisation. In Ireland there are almost 300,000 unemployed, in Britain 3 million, in the European Union 17 to 18 million. Many of these are long-term. Some have never worked at all. Some of the younger people will never have a job in their life-time. And this is the more developed and traditionally Christian part of the world. Yet the economic and political system requires the exclusion of so many people from their right to work as recognised in the United Nations Charter, and from exercising their God-given vocation to be co-creators of their world. Can the eucharist be celebrated in such circumstances without the excluders, the people of economic and political power, eating and drinking judgement on themselves? How can the unemployed be honestly asked to join in celebrating a liturgy from whose preparation in the work of human hands they have been systematically excluded?

Sharing the Meal

Divine and human collaboration is always moving beyond the production of food and drink to the creation of a meal, a community event at once celebratory and nourishing. Eucharist is also such an event but, in its fuller meaning as eating and drinking bread and wine become body and blood of Christ, it symbolises the sharing of all humanity in the life-giving gifts of God, including the gift of Godself. Worthy celebration of the eucharist must again take seriously the full range of its symbolism. The earth and its fruits are for all. The work of human hands and hearts and minds must seek, in imitation of the Creator, to ensure this. The eucharist summons Christians to give a lead and play their part in ensuring this. The meal-ministry of Jesus in feeding the hungry and in eating and drinking with sinners and the excluded, provides the background to his farewell meal with his disciples, the origin of our eucharist. The prophetic questions must once again be voiced. How can we celebrate eucharist in a world of recurring famine and permanent food mountains and wine lakes? In a world where a billion people live in absolute poverty? In a world where a million children under five die every month in the countries of the South? Given the existing awareness, resources, technology and means of distribution, does the continuing inactivity of the powerful and secure amount to a passive form of genocide? Can we Christians celebrate eucharist in a genocidal world in which we are at least passive participants?

The prophetic character of the eucharist inheres in its very sacramentality. The symbolic recognition and celebration include protest and judgement. They summon to resistance and transformation. The range of that summons to judgement and transformation extends, as we have seen, beyond the *domus Dei* and its individual members or believers to the *mundus Dei*, the natural and human worlds of God. The role of the *domus Dei*, of the church and of its sacraments is to recognise and promote the transformation of the *mundus Dei* into the *regnum Dei*. From creation to new creation through the coming of the kingdom is the gift and call of Jesus' redemptive life and death. The church operates as midwife in this further exercise of divine creativity.

The church is also under judgement, summoned to transformation itself. In its teaching and living it frequently fails to reflect what it celebrates in eucharist. Its service to the *regnum Dei*, to the coming of God's kingdom, is thereby diminished. Too often in past and present, the church's explicit or implicit alignment with oppressive powers has contradicted its sacramental enactment of the liberating presence and power of God. Despite all the declarations of fine intentions in papal encyclicals and bishops' pastorals, and the heroic service of so many religious and lay communities and individuals, the church community constantly stands in need of judgement and conversion. Sometimes the call to judgement may arise outside the church itself. The *mundus Dei* and its apparent unbelievers may be closer to the *regnum Dei* than the *domus Dei* and its apparent believers. Movement by the Spirit is not limited to the confines of the visible church. Creation and the large human community may be at times more effective signs of the coming of the kingdom. Formal and valid sacraments may be frustrated by ecclesial blindness and weakness.

Oppression of women has for too long been a counter-sign of the coming kingdom in church as well as society. Indeed the church has had to learn from the broader movement towards women's liberation about the extent of that oppression and the need to overcome it. Jesus' exemplary relations with women, as recorded in the gospels, seem to have been obscured over the centuries. The eucharist call for an inclusive society beyond oppressive divisions, including that of male and female (Gal 3:28), is still far from realisation. As symbolic meal, underlining the communion aspects of all meals and human gatherings, the eucharist calls attention to the nurturing and gathering role which women have historically fulfiled. In any future debates about women's role in the celebration of the eucharist, their role at family meals of gathering the family, preparing and serving food may be ignored only at the expense of the very symbol and sacrament itself.

Celebration and prophecy

The celebratory character of the eucharist should never be obscured. In the context of creation, it echoes God rejoicing in the creation and the creation rejoicing in its God. The 'Mass on the World' vision of Teilhard de Chardin expresses all that magnificently. There remains the judgement and the protest, the 'Mass for hard times' as R. S. Thomas called it. His critical and prophetic vision is finally centred on the cross. Mass is a sacrifice, Christ's sacrifice re-membered and re-presented. So much of Catholic theology has concentrated on this aspect for so long that the very 'celebration' rang hollow and the social critique was entirely obscured. Yet without the cross the Mass would not be the Mass. In a world of war and pestilence and starvation, where the slow torture of God and humanity continues as on Calvary, the crucified God is remembered and made present as crucified and identified with all the victims of history. It is also the risen crucified who receives us and whom we receive. Resurrection is cause for celebration but is only available to us, as it was to Jesus, by taking on the suffering of the world.

The sign of the cross can be used to oppress rather than to liberate. Preoccupation with the deaths on the cross can become depressing and escapist. Resurrection can be too easily displaced to the end-time. Many Christians, not all women, would welcome more emphasis on birth than on death. New creation is one among many such life-giving images in the New Testament of which 'being born again' is the most obvious. The mystery and the paradox of the life-giving death of Jesus as made present in the eucharist do not yield to systematic explanation. Eliot's Magi might have had some illuminating comment if they had gone to Calvary rather than to Bethlehem. It may not be impertinent to para- or re-phrase them here:

Were we led all that way for
Death or Birth? There was a Death, certainly.
We had evidence and no doubt. I had seen death and birth,
But had thought they were different ...

Eucharist is death and birth, fearsome prophecy and joyous celebration.

Otherness in Communion

The mystery and paradox of the eucharist inevitably reflect the
mystery and paradox of human existence and, more broadly still,
those of the Creator-creation relationship. The otherness characteristic of that relationship, the developing otherness internal to creation itself, and the modes of otherness inherent in human relationships, transcend our human understanding. In their opacity they
signal the fragility of all cosmic and human reality. No thing or person, relationship or community, is assured of stability or permanence. The contingency of creaturehood in all its forms and relationships is a matter of everyday experience. Otherness, contingency and their associate, discontinuity, offer a serious challenge to
any prospect of community or communion including eucharistic or
holy communion.

The assumption of easy communion is deep-rooted in human
relationships. Families, neighbours, whole societies and even
churches, presume a certain community and solidarity and are
often surprised when hostile divisions emerge. That human
assumption has its cosmic and even divine analogues. Break-down
and division in rock-solid geological formations, or the flood of nor-
mally trustworthy rivers, may suddenly distress human and other
inhabitants. The history of God's relationship with humanity is a
history of breakdown and distress. God's last hurrah, as it were, in
sending God's Son to establish or re-establish community with
God's chosen people was apparently no more successful than a long
list of previous ones. 'This is the heir ... let us kill him and the vine-
yard will be ours' (Mk 12:1ff). The meal-communities which Jesus
established with prostitutes and sinners, tax-collectors and other
socially excluded people, alienated the religious leaders. His
bypassing the Sabbath regulations to heal the sick and feed the hungry offended their sense of the holiness/otherness of God. His
claim to overcome the deepest estrangements of all in forgiving sin
appeared to them as outright blasphemy. It was an assumption of
identity with the divine unnameable Holy One, the ultimate Other.

Jesus' rejection by his people, his betrayal by one of the twelve whom he called personally, his desertion by the others, his condemnation to death by the religious and political authorities and his execution outside the gates of the city as a criminal, completed the hostile othering. He was excluded from all community as totally estranged and so dehumanised. The attempts at divine-human communion seem to have finally broken down. Divine and human otherness are no longer open to communion. Discontinuity between God and humanity, as between humans themselves, prevails. Even the dying Jesus cries out, 'My God, my God, why have you forsaken me?' (Mt 27:47).

The estrangement of Jesus, the model of love, in life and death, exposes the range of hostile and destructive division and discontinuity in society and cosmos. Without understanding that, without recognising our own complicity in it, we cannot hope to go, or better to be taken, beyond it. 'Beyond estrangement' becomes possible for humanity and cosmos in the gracious raising of Jesus from the dead. It becomes accessible in every place and time because on the night before he died:

> As they were eating, Jesus took bread and blessed and broke it, and gave it to his disciples and said, 'Take, eat, this is my body'. And he took a cup, and when he had given thanks he gave it to them, saying, 'Drink of it, all of you; for this is my blood of the covenant, which is poured out for many for the forgiveness of sins' (Mt 26:26-28).

The holy communion, which the eucharist promises and anticipates, involves the disorientation of Calvary. Only those who recognise and take on board the estrangement and discontinuity which Jesus experience on the cross can truly enter into new communion with God, neighbour and cosmos. The created otherness and differentiation which, in origins and potential reflect the gracious and enriching gifts of the Creator, still loom threateningly over our world. The crucifixion-resurrection of Jesus exposes both the depth of the threat and the triumph of the gift. A true and holy communion of others in Jesus is what eucharist symbolises and realises. The new creation, however fragile and limited, is emerging in the sharing of bread and wine by his instructions and in his memory. Creator, creation and humanity enjoy new hope of otherness in communion in which differentiation will provide deeper bonds for communication rather than fresh sources of discontinuity and division.